THE JOURNAL OF THE

C. I. V.

IN SOUTH AFRICA

CROSSING THE VAAL AT VILLIERSDORP

Frontispiece　　　　　　　　　　　　　*Photo by Major Pawle*

THE JOURNAL OF THE C. I. V. IN SOUTH AFRICA

By MAJOR-GEN. W. H. MACKINNON
COMMANDANT OF THE CORPS

WITH PLANS AND ILLUSTRATIONS

LONDON
JOHN MURRAY, ALBEMARLE STREET, W.
1901

DEDICATED

TO OUR COLONEL

FIELD-MARSHAL

EARL ROBERTS

*War Office, London,
13th February, 1901.*

Dear General Mackinnon,—I very gladly accept the dedication of your Journal of the C.I.V. in South Africa, and I am very glad to think that this interesting record of the corps, of which I had the honour to be Honorary Colonel, is to be published.—Believe me, yours very truly,

ROBERTS.

PREFACE

ORIGINALLY intended for private circulation only, this Journal has been published at the request of many members of the Regiment.

It has been kept regularly from day to day, and the distances, &c., have been checked with the notes made by Staff and other Officers.

It was matter for great regret that the three parts of the Regiment were, owing to the exigencies of the service, so scattered, and, in consequence, this book deals chiefly with the Infantry battalion, with which the Commandant was mostly associated.

A complete roll of the whole corps is given, which it is thought may be of interest.

My acknowledgments and thanks are due to Messrs. Underwood & Underwood, London, for permission to reproduce their copyright stereoscopic photographs, and also to Captain J. Orr and Mr. L. Green Wilkinson for assistance in the preparation of the book.

CONTENTS

CHAP.		PAGE
I.	RAISING OF REGIMENT—VOYAGE OUT	1
II.	LINES OF COMMUNICATION	26
III.	ORANGE RIVER TO THE VAAL	48
IV.	FIGHT AT DOORN KOP	74
V.	DOORN KOP TO PRETORIA	82
VI.	ROUND PRETORIA	89
VII.	DIAMOND HILL	95
VIII.	BACK TO PRETORIA	101
IX.	TO HEIDELBERG	107
X.	HEIDELBERG TO HEILBRON	115
XI.	AT HEILBRON	123
XII.	HEILBRON TO FREDERICKSTADT	142
XIII.	AT FREDERICKSTADT	147
XIV.	BETWEEN FREDERICKSTADT AND BANK	156
XV.	WITH KITCHENER AFTER DE WET	160
XVI.	LORD ALBEMARLE'S MOVEMENT	172
XVII.	AT PRETORIA FOR THE THIRD TIME	186
XVIII.	HOME	207

CONTENTS

APPENDICES

	PAGE
A.—Analysis of Trades	221
B.—State of Various Detachments comprising Infantry Battalion	223
C.—Earl Roberts' Farewell Address	224
D.—List of Camps	227
E.—Number of Courts-Martial in the Regiment during the Campaign	229
F.—Return of 99 Cases of Enteric Fever contracted on Service in South Africa, February to October 1900	229
G.—Return of 104 Cases of Enteric Fever contracted on Service in South Africa, February to November 1, 1900, including those which occurred on the Homeward Voyage	230
H.—Nominal Roll of the Regiment	231
I.—Nominal Roll of the Draft	250
K.—Number of Officers and Men who Served in South Africa	252

LIST OF ILLUSTRATIONS

Crossing the Vaal at Villiersdorp	*Frontispiece*	
Group of C.I.V.'s	to face page	26
Our Maxims	,,	38
Wrecked Bridge at Norval's Pont	,,	44
Our Water-Cart	,,	64
Crossing Rhenoster River	,,	70
(1) In Camp. (2) Diamond Hill, First Day. (3) Diamond Hill, the Artillery going into Action	,,	96
Diamond Hill. Part of the Boer Final Position from Within	,,	98
Some of the Cyclist Section	,,	118
Our Ambulance	,,	128
Evacuating Heilbron	,,	140
Wrecked Train, Frederickstadt. Steam still issuing from Funnel	,,	146
Our Stretcher-Bearers	,,	150
Waiting the Order to Dismiss	,,	170
C.I.V.'s Shedding Tears (Peeling Onions)	,,	180
Transport by Train	,,	206

MAPS AND PLANS

BATTLE OF DOORNKOP . . . . *page* 81

DIAMOND HILL . . . . . *to face page* 100

> From Mr. Winston Churchill's account of the battle, by permission of Messrs. Longman & Co. and the proprietors of the *Morning Post*.

MAP TO ILLUSTRATE THE MARCH OF THE
INFANTRY BATTALION OF THE C.I.V. *to face page* 116

THE JOURNAL OF THE C.I.V. IN SOUTH AFRICA

CHAPTER I

RAISING OF REGIMENT—VOYAGE OUT

[At this time Buller had been checked at Colenso, Methuen at Magersfontein, and Gatacre at Stormberg, and there was a feeling of depression in England, though not in any way one of despair.]

On December 22, 1899, I was summoned to the War Office, and was offered by Lord Wolseley the command of the City Imperial Volunteers, which I accepted. The Lord Mayor had previously been to the Commander-in-Chief, and had offered to raise a regiment of infantry, with mounted infantry attached; to clothe, equip, and transport them by sea to

Cape Town, where they were to be taken over by the War Office. This offer had been accepted, the Commander-in-Chief reserving to himself the right to nominate the Lieutenant-Colonels and certain of the officers.

Colonel Cholmondeley and Sir Howard Vincent were the two Lieutenant-Colonels appointed; but the latter officer failing to pass the medical examination, Colonel the Earl of Albemarle was selected in his place to command the infantry, the command of the mounted infantry being intrusted to Colonel Cholmondeley.

From Christmas till the end of the year preparations were made for accepting the services of the required number of men from the list of those volunteering.

January 1, 1900.—On this day 365 men were sworn in at the Guildhall by the Lord Mayor and five aldermen and sheriffs. Leave was given for the H.A.C. to send a field-battery to join the regiment.

January 4, 1900.—900 more men were sworn in at the Guildhall. About 80 men of the H.A.C. were sworn in at Finsbury, and also

15 or 20 details for the remainder of the regiment

January 11.—General Trotter, commanding the Home District, inspected the mounted infantry at the Drill Hall, Bunhill Row.

January 12.—Clothing and equipping the 500 men for embarkation to-morrow were carried on all day at the Guildhall; all ranks received the Freedom of the City of London, the presentation of which to the officers was made with much ceremony and picturesqueness, in the presence of the Duke of Cambridge. The men also drew their rifles from the Tower. At 8 P.M. the detachment attended a farewell service in St. Paul's, subsequently marching through dense masses of people to the Temple, where they were entertained at supper by the Inner Temple. The enthusiasm of the populace was very marked, and the formation of the ranks could not be kept. After supper the detachment returned to Bunhill Row, where they slept.

January 13.—The detachment marched out of Bunhill Row at 7 A.M., but, owing to the enormous crowds lining the streets, it took three hours and twenty minutes, instead of seventy minutes, to get to Nine Elms. Several of the men were exhausted, and many articles of equipment were lost.

The detachment arrived at Southampton at 12.45, and immediately embarked; 250 on the *Briton* under Colonel Cholmondeley, and 250 on the *Garth Castle* under Captain Shipley. Both these ships sailed during the afternoon.

January 17.—The 800 men for embarkation next Saturday received their boots and rifles to-day from the Guildhall and Tower respectively, and were also presented with the Freedom of the City of London.

January 19.—They were clothed and equipped at the Guildhall, and took up quarters at the two drill halls in James Street, whence they marched at 6.45 P.M. to St. Paul's, where a very impressive farewell service was held, the Bishop of London giving a short address. Thence they marched through crowded streets to Gray's Inn, which took in 200, the remaining 600 proceeding to Lincoln's Inn. After supper, which had been generously provided by the Benchers, the whole detachment marched back to James Street and slept there. Rain fell heavily.

January 20.—The detachment marched by companies at 6.30 A.M. to Wellington Barracks, where they had breakfast: leaving there at 7.30 A.M., they arrived at Nine Elms at 8.30 A.M. Much enthusiasm was shown, especially near Westminster Bridge. H.R.H. the Duke of Connaught was present to see the detachment start. The two specials left at 8.45 A.M. and 8.55 A.M., arriving at Southampton in 2½ hours, where C., D., F., and H. Companies embarked on the *Ariosto*, A. on the *Gaul*, and B. and part of C. on the *Kinfauns Castle*. It rained heavily all the morning and during the embarkation. The *Ariosto* sailed at 2.15 P.M.

January 21.—After passing the Needles the sea became choppy, and most of the officers and men succumbed. There was a decided roll on all day. I held divine service in the saloon at 11 A.M., which was attended by eight officers and about twenty-five men. Most of the officers were ill, Captain Edis, Lieutenant Green and myself appearing to be the best sailors. Distance run up to noon 246 miles, which was very good, considering that we only started at 2.15 P.M. yesterday, and did not go "full speed" till 3.15.

January 22.—Still a nasty Atlantic roll on, with a head-wind; but a bit of sun cheered the men, though they lay like logs most of the day. Did not attempt to get any parade out of them. I asked a sentry what his profession was, and he replied, "I have none, sir, but my amusement in life is archæology, and I was going this very week to Athens and the Levant."

Run up to noon, 249 miles. Wind and sea going down. Weather milder.

January 23.—A lovely morning, with a slight S.E. breeze. Sea calm. A morning worth waking for, and truly, as a Western cowboy once said to me, "God's own private morning, sure." Quite a different look on all faces to-day.

Had a general parade at 9.30 A.M. to get all ranks out, the orderly men meantime cleaning up all the quarters. At 11.30, the sergeant-major drilled the officers in physical drill, and, at another time, he drilled the sergeants. Seeing one of the latter very steady on his pins, I inquired about him, and ascertained that he was the possessor of a yacht of his own. The drill was not very impressive, as standing on tip-toe is not easy during the first few days at sea, even in smooth water. We are now hovering between Europe and Africa. Run up to noon, 283 miles. Wind light. Sea calm.

At 2 P.M. I start a class in Dutch, Bellairs of the cyclist section being instructor.

Captain Newman is very agreeable, and as his usual runs are to Russia and Sweden, he tells me much of countries of which I know very little.

January 24.—Sick report, six men. Nothing serious. One case of erysipelas from a fall on deck, one suffering from alcohol, for which some of his send-offs are responsible; certainly *not* the ship; for although mistaken friends have sent me over 2000 bottles of whisky, and enough beer to give each man five gallons, it is locked up, and only issued under strict supervision, one pint of beer at noon, and a "tot" of whisky at 8 P.M. Out of our 500 men 147 are teetotallers.

Very close this morning, as we are in the N.E. trades, which are moving in the same direction as we are.

Two complaints to-day, (1) insufficient washing accommodation; (2) the dry canteen not open long enough. Have inquired into both. The former will be remedied to-morrow by the hose being turned on early each morning, and the latter is already rectified.

I find some of the volunteer sergeants very deficient in the knowledge of how to instruct, or even *drill* their men without instruction; and *some* of the men are ignorant of the most elementary knowledge of drill. I am sure we must make the sergeants efficient first, and I have started sergeants' classes, at which each one will be taught *how* to *call out* his words of command; if they can once get confidence in that, they will soon become of value. The conversational style in which some of them give commands to strong squads of men is not conducive to efficiency. I look for *great* improvement, as they are all intelligent and all willing. Have told off Mr. Green to look after the musketry instruction.

The run to-day was 296 miles, the wind N.E., light, sea calm. About 7 P.M. a fine flying-fish came on board, and was caught.

January 25.—We sighted Madeira at 6.30 A.M., but there was a haze on. We passed abeam of it, to the west, at 9 A.M., ten miles distant, the haze making the hills look very high.

Everything at full pressure to-day, and a capital sail bath, with hose turned on from 6–7 A.M., was a success. The sergeant-major drills the officers daily at physical drill, and they quite like it. I fell in with them the first day. Sun is hot, and I have issued an order that no man is to appear on deck during the daytime without a covering to his head. Run up to noon, 280 miles. Wind N.E., fresh, with quite a roll on.

The list of officers, up to date of embarking, which has been approved by the War Office as notified to me by telegram, was as follows :—

Colonel-Commandant . . . . W. H. MacKinnon
Orderly Officer . Capt. E. H. Trotter, Grenadier Guards
Transport Officer . . . . Capt. J. E. H. Orr
Paymaster . . . . Capt. Triggs, late A.P.D.
Medical Officer . . . . . Surgeon-Capt. R. R. Sleman
Veterinary Officer . . . . Lieut. W. S. Mulvey

FIELD BATTERY

Major G. M'Micking
Capt. E. C. Budworth
Lieut. A. C. Lowe

Lieut. H. Bayley
Lieut. L. F. Duncan
Surg.-Capt. A. Thorne

MOUNTED INFANTRY

Commanding . . . . Lieut.-Col. H. C. Cholmondeley
Adjutant . . . . Capt. E. Bell
Quartermaster . . . . Capt. J. Ridler

No. 1 Company

Capt. J. W. Reid
Lieut. G. Berry

Lieut. W. H. Brailey
Lieut. B. Moëller

Lieut. C. H. W. Wilson

No. 2 Company

Capt. J. F. Waterlow
Lieut. E. G. Concannon
Lieut. A. H. Henderson
Lieut. E. A. Manisty

Lieut. A. Bailey (now in South Africa, a commission to be offered to him).

MACHINE-GUN SECTION . . . . . Lieut. E. V. Welby

INFANTRY

Lieut.-Colonel . . . . Earl of Albemarle
Second in Command . . . . . . Major A. G. Pawle
Adjutant . . Capt. Hon. J. R. Bailey, Grenadier Guards

A. Company

Capt. A. Reid   Lieut. F. R. Jeffery
Lieut. E. D. Townroe

B. Company

Capt. C. W. Berkeley   Lieut. W. B. Garnett
Lieut. J. W. Cohen

C. Company

Capt. C. G. R. Matthey   Lieut. Hon. S. M'Donnell, C.B.
Lieut. E. Treffry

D. Company

Capt. F. J. Cousens   Lieut. J. H. Smith
Lieut. S. R. Burnside

E. Company

Capt. R. B. Shipley   Lieut. W. J. P. Benson
Lieut. F. B. Marsh

F. Company

Capt. W. Edis   Lieut. P. F. Brown
Lieut. S. H. Hole

G. Company

Capt. A. A. Howell   Lieut. C. P. Grindle
Lieut. P. Croft

H. Company

Capt. C. A. Mortimore   Lieut. W. B. L. Alt
Lieut. B. C. Green

Quartermaster . . . . Capt. S. Firth
Medical Officer . . . . Surgeon-Capt. E. St. V. Ryan
(This officer was with the Mounted Infantry throughout the campaign.)

Captain Sleman inoculated about four officers and fifty men to-day.

January 26.—Lovely morning, with wind a good deal gone down. The captain, at my request, inspected the men's quarters, and was pleased with them. The inoculation patients have suffered a good deal of pain; the men, especially, have a great thirst. Run up to noon, 288 miles.

We began musketry drill. The volunteer sergeants are improving daily in their words of command, and also in their ability to impart instruction.

January 27.—Warm to-day, though the breeze is pleasant. The inoculated officers and men are all out of bed, though they are not yet fit for duty. The captain inspected the hospital, &c., and saw the convalescents. Lime-juice was issued to all hands. Began rifle drill. We met a large four-masted steamer yesterday evening homeward-bound, also the *Min*, a London "tramp."

Run up to 12 noon was 293½ miles. Lovely night, with the heavens one mass of stars. Southern cross visible.

January 28.—Passed a tramp quite close at 7 A.M., men cheering her loudly. She blew her steam siren in reply. At 11 o'clock I held divine service on the quarter-deck, the whole detachment attending.

Run up to noon, 288 miles. We sighted San Antonio about 7 P.M., and came to an anchor at St. Vincent at 11 P.M. Too late to get pratique, but we opened lamp signalling with H.M.S. *Cambrian*, and got the latest war news.

January 29.—Doctor came on board at 7 A.M., and the agent at 8 A.M., bringing me two cables, one dated London, 27, 5.25 P.M.: "If possible, return by mail duplicate attestations and regimental roll, if available. War Office continually asking for details we cannot give. Adjutant-General has approved helmets for whole force. These will be shipped shortly.—Boxall." The other was dated, also London, 27, 5.25 P.M.: "Authorities have cabled Lord Roberts to have everything ready until our own camp equipment and transport details arrive at Cape Town. I have agreed, at authorities' request, to provide these, and camp equipment goes *Pembroke Castle* to-day. All officers gazetted.—Newton, L. Mayor."

An officer of H.M.S. *Cambrian* came on board at 8.30 A.M., and offered us any assistance we might want. I called on the captain (Macalpine) at 10.15 A.M. with Trotter and Firth, and we subsequently went on the transport *City of Rome*, which has two batteries of artillery and two militia battalions on board. I found many friends, including Sir C. Parsons, R.A., commanding the troops; Colonel Dick, commanding the Argyll and Sutherland Militia; also Tom Cochrane, one of his captains; and Napier, another captain.

Returned on board, and was busy all day getting attestations ready, excepting a hurried visit ashore to send two telegrams: (1) to the Lord Mayor, "Cable received. All well;" and (2) to Colonel Boxall, saying the attestations and roll were going by this mail. I also sent a message to Burroughs & Welcome, London, asking for medical stores for Sleman. St. Vincent reminds me somewhat of Skye and the West Coast of Scotland. I did not allow the men ashore, as

Captain Macalpine strongly advised me not to; the bluejackets and marines are not allowed to go, and the *City of Rome* gave no leave. I am sorry for our men, but am sure it was for the best. Parsons, Macalpine, Leveson-Gower, and another lieutenant (H.M.S. *Cambrian*), and Tom Cochrane dined with me on the *Ariosto*, and we gave them quite a good dinner.

I received the following cable this afternoon: " London, 29, 1.50 P.M.—Army order of Saturday calls in Lee-Enfields, similar yours, because sighting defective, as we knew. Can we usefully do anything now?—Boxall." This is annoying, as it tends to create want of confidence among men who, above all else, are good shots and fond of their rifles. I specially asked for new rifles for this regiment, thinking that we should get the very best, and that some of those which were in the hands of the men at the time of enrolment might be in some way or other defective; also because the great majority of rifles of the Home District volunteers were at Weedon for examination, and could not possibly be back in time. And this is the result! However, it is the only part of our outfit which has proved defective.

January 30.—Heavy rain this morning. We sent our mail—two large sacks—to the *Cambrian* for transfer to the homeward mail steamer.

Got off all the attestations, Sergeant Hall, assisted by others, sitting up the whole night to finish them. I am retaining here as many duplicate attestations as I have got, and have asked General Trotter to cause the missing ones to be sent me.

Coaling, which had gone on all night, finished at 10 A.M.; then water was put on board, and we weighed anchor at 11.30, leaving St. Vincent for our long voyage to Cape Town. We were heartily cheered by the *Cambrian*, *City of Rome*, and several English merchant ships.

At 6 P.M. Sleman begins a course of preparation for inoculation for myself, Trotter, four other officers and some ninety non-commissioned officers and men. Alt gave us a capital concert to-night, with some good glees;

and Walker, my orderly, danced and played the violin. There was also a good foursome reel.

January 31.—Last night was very hot, but there is a nice breeze to-day. A steamer crossed our bows at 9.30 A.M. going west, probably from Las Palmas to Brazil. Run up to noon, 244 miles, which disappoints the captain, who says it is due to the Welsh coal we took on at St. Vincent, the ship's furnaces being constructed for North Country coal. I saw the sergeants at 5 P.M., and read to them extracts from the Queen's Regulations.

At 6 P.M. Sleman ran his needle in, and the subsequent proceedings of the *Ariosto* did not interest me!

February 1.—Run up to noon, 240 miles. A great deal of motion. Strong north-east wind. I was in bed all day; not much pain, but intense weakness; temperature $102\frac{1}{2}$.

February 2.—Allowed up after breakfast; very weak, with a good deal of pain in loins, but getting perceptibly better.

Run to-day, 251 miles. Still too rough for men to drill with rifles. Quartermaster's heart rejoiced by finding his marking equipment in the hold. Began marking men's kits at once.

February 3.—Finer weather, but hot. Run up to noon, 252 miles.

Put in a useful day's work; drill up to 3 P.M., then a fire alarm; then I read the Mutiny Act to the men, and gave them a short lecture on the necessity of at once complying with all orders. If they think an order wrong, to obey it first, and to ask to see their captain afterwards. All orders given by an authorised person, whether by myself, a lance-corporal, a sentry, or a provost, must be at once attended to without argument. If a man comes into camp from a long march, wet through, tired, and longing for his dinner, and is ordered off by a corporal on water fatigue, he must go. There will be many other days on which the sun will shine for him. I then explained the mode of redress of grievances. If not satisfied with the captain's decision, a soldier can ask to see his commanding officer, and if, unhappily, he is not satisfied then, he is entitled to see the General commanding, although I hoped it would never come to that; still, as we require implicit obedience from them, I was glad to show them what safeguards the law provides to ensure that they should have justice.

Afterwards I had the various bugle-calls blown, so that they might learn them; then an hour's examination of the officers on infantry drill. Satisfactory; they had evidently read their books carefully. Then we had an hour's interesting talk over camp life, cooking, probable plan of campaign, &c.

Fifty more men volunteer to-day for inoculation.

The captain having consented, all men sleep on deck, much to their joy. The heat is great, and they are beginning to suffer from œdema, &c., so we have knocked off the morning beer and the evening "tot," and issue lime-juice daily. This, and the sleeping on deck and the morning douche, will brace them up. We are now in the Doldrums, and there is very little wind. I slept on deck.

February 4.—The first really calm day for some time, and it is a great relief. What wind there is shifted about midnight to south-west. Sleeping on deck, one could revel in the stars—such stars—and in such numbers!

Held divine service at 11 A.M. Men very responsive. Hymns, "Hark, hark, my soul," and "Eternal Father." M'Donnell read the Lesson for me, as I found the strain on my voice trying after my inoculation. The captain and his officers and crew attended service. I spoke to our men afterwards, urging them—especially the younger ones—to get inoculated. I told them it was no doctor's fad, but a medical fact that, if they submitted, they would run less chance of suffering from the one disease in South Africa which is so detrimental to the health of the troops. I also pointed out to them that their going to hospital would impair the efficiency of the battalion, not to speak of the injury that might be done to their own health.

During service we crossed the Line.

Run up to noon was 240 miles.

The first officer gave us a display of rockets after dinner.

February 5.—A lovely day with a cooling head wind. Run up to noon, 249 miles.

The Welsh coal we took on at St. Vincent is entirely responsible for our reduced speed, as the weather is far the best we have had. Cousens is still unwell, and has hardly been fit for duty since we sailed.

We did revolver practice to-day, six shots each at a mark. I began the practice, and luckily made a hit the first shot, though I missed all the others. The sergeant-major and the sergeant-cook did the best.

We had a concert to-night, at which Green and Alt sang. Amongst the items were two glees, very prettily sung by some of the cyclist section and others. There were also a reel and three rounds of boxing.

Nights are very lovely, with a good moon coming on.

February 6.—The run up to noon was 237 miles. We had a useful day's work, as, after our ordinary morning parades, we put the cyclists, signallers, and part of C. Company through some musketry, letting them all shoot sectional practices out to sea with ball cartridge. It is curious how little the volunteers know about the service rifle; not one in fifty knows anything about the charging or the management of the magazine; and frequently, when I see a man a perfect incubus to his section owing to his ignorance of sectional practices, I find on inquiry that he is a prize shot at Bisley. However, if such men can be made good sectional shots, they will be doubly useful to the regiment.

Sleman and no fewer than 152 men were inoculated to-night. Very good of them to come forward in such numbers after what I said to them on Sunday.

February 7.—We did some more sectional practice with ball cartridge to-day. Saw several flying-fish, and, for the first time, a shark. Cooler, and doctor sanctions re-issue of beer and the evening "tot." Run up to noon, 256 miles.

February 8.—Heavy rain early, and atmosphere still cooler. Run up to noon, 257 miles. Went through men's kits, and decided on what they will put in sea-kit bag, kit bag, valise, and haversack respectively.

February 9.—Nice busy day. First parade 7 A.M., and fully occupied up till 6 P.M. Had all the detachment on parade at intervals in heavy marching order. Also did some more sectional practice with ball cartridge. Disappointed in this, as there is a lamentable ignorance of fire discipline, and I am continually finding crack Bisley shots who spoil their section's shooting, and, what is more remarkable, these men seem to be the most nervous of all the rank and file. I don't mind these good shots having unmilitary positions; I don't object to their wearing glasses, nor to their blacking their sights; but I cannot stand their ignorance of the use of the magazine, or of the elementary rules for the management and handling of the rifle. I have had to order several men extra practice.

Our run was 257 miles. Shortly before noon we passed within a mile of the *Kildonan Castle*, homeward bound. She signalled, "No news. Buller advancing."

February 10.—Strong head wind. Run only 226 miles. Parades on nearly all day. Passed Union Liner homeward bound at 11.40 P.M., with whom we exchanged night signals.

February 11.—Had church parade at 11; as usual a delightful service. Hymns were "O Paradise" and "The Church's one Foundation." Spent all the rest of the day in sorting War Office forms, stationery, &c.

Sleman gives me the numbers who have been inoculated, which come out at 72.70 per cent. of those on board. Run to-day, 247 miles.

February 12.—Cooler this morning, after a very rolly night. Run was 252 miles. Had a general parade to try and find missing valises. Shot D. Company in the afternoon.

February 13.—Had our usual parades. Run, 268 miles. Put the subaltern officers through the firing exercise with ball cartridge.

February 14.—Blowing hard from south with heavy sea. Run, 245 miles. Went round ship, but could not have parades.

February 15.—A good deal of motion all night. Run up to noon, 215 miles. Sighted the high land near Saldanha Bay at 12.45 P.M. Clear sky but fresh breeze. Passed mail-steamer of Castle Line about mid-day, homeward bound.

The sight of Table Bay and Mountain is most impressive; the latter had the tablecloth spread. We came slowly in by Robben Island, where we gave our number, and came to anchor about a mile off the dock at 6 P.M. Newton and Mr. Watson came off to see us. We were delighted to hear that the mounted infantry had gone up to the front.

February 16.—Got into dock at 10 A.M., passing many transports, including the *Umbria*. We landed at 11 A.M., everything quiet and orderly, and marched to Green Point Camp (1½ miles), where we found E. Company and mounted infantry details. I called on the General (Walker) and the chief staff officer (Cooper), and saw many friends, including Joey Davies, Walter and Jos Bagot, and Algy Lennox.

CHAPTER II

LINES OF COMMUNICATION

[THERE had been no material change in Natal since we left England, but Kimberley was relieved by French on 15th February.]

February 17.—It blew a hurricane last night; my tent curtain was repeatedly blown in, and I did not sleep at all.

Saw battalion at various kinds of drill, and busy all day marking kits, sorting out stores, &c. Very glad to hear that we shall probably move on Tuesday.

Find Mr. Abe Bailey invaluable; he is very practical, helpful, and knows everybody. I lunched with Algy Lennox. A good many of us dined with Newton at his hotel to meet the Mayor. Appointed Private Baillie a lieutenant in the Mounted Infantry, as, to my regret, I found it impossible to persuade Mr.

GROUP OF C.I.V.'S

Photo by Underwood & Underwood

To face p. 26

Abe Bailey to accept a commission. He is one of the Edinburgh contingent, and gives every sign of being likely to become an efficient officer. Dined with Newton at Mount Nelson Hotel.

February 18.—We attended brigade church parade.

A man arrived this morning from New Zealand: he is a Londoner, and belongs to the Hon. Artillery Company. He cabled from New Zealand to his commanding officer, and was advised to meet me here, and, coming at his own expense, has just hit us off. I attested him at once.

Orders received to prepare to move headquarters and six companies on Tuesday next to Orange River, and the details of mounted infantry to Stellenbosch on Monday.

Lunched with Algy Lennox, and went to see W. Lambton at Mr. Rhodes's house. Dined with Mr. Abe Bailey.

February 19.—Orders received to-day that we cannot be taken north to-morrow, but are to be in readiness to move on Wednesday to Orange River (this was subsequently altered to Naauwpoort). Busy day for quartermaster, issuing deficiencies in kits, marking, &c.

The *Pembroke Castle* arrived to-day, and 120 men of G. Company marched into camp under Major Pawle. The officers accompanying him were Lieutenant Croft and Lieutenant Grindle; the latter had to go straight to Wynberg Hospital from the ship, suffering from debility. At 5 P.M. the Mayor and a few other gentlemen came to camp to welcome the regiment formally; the men fell in in front of their tents, and the party went down each line, and expressed admiration of their appearance. The Corporation sent an immense present of fruit, cheeses, and butter to the regiment, accompanied by a kindly worded official letter. The Governor, Sir A. Milner, with whom I lunched yesterday, was complimentary about the turn-out of the men, especially when on sentry-go at Government House, where we find the guard daily.

I see a good deal of Mr. Abe Bailey, who is most helpful in every way.

The details of our mounted infantry left

LINES OF COMMUNICATION

camp to-day for Stellenbosch by march route, the dismounted party going by rail.

February 20.—Paraded at 8.30 A.M. for a brigade march through Cape Town; the streets were crowded and decorated. On return to camp, I found a telegram from the railway staff officer, asking if we could conveniently entrain this afternoon: sent Trotter to him to arrange whatever might best suit public service.

Albemarle and I lunched with the Mayor and Council at the City Club. Speeches were made; in mine, I dwelt on the great loyalty of the citizens of London. Trotter came during lunch, and reported that it would be most convenient for every one that we should go north to-morrow.

On our return to camp, I found a telegram from the chief staff officer saying we were to go north—20 officers and between 600 and 700 men—to-night, taking only tents and blankets. Paraded at 6.45 P.M., and found on arrival at the railway station that the train did not leave till 9.55 P.M. Bailey and Trotter accompany me, also Newton and Watson, for whom I have special permits. A., B., C., E., and F. are the Companies. We left at 10, and at midnight part of the train ran off the line; no one was hurt. We were delayed six hours.

February 21.—Stopped at Worcester for breakfast, at Tows River for dinner, and at Matjesfontein for tea—arrangements very good. At the last place we saw, just outside the town, the monument erected to General Wauchope by Mr. Logan, who lives here, and who entertained all the officers at dinner. Met Ellison (2nd Life Guards) proceeding sick to Cape Town.

The scenery by the Hex River was very grand, and our climb of 1400 feet necessitated three engines—two in front, and one behind. Our strength is 702, all ranks, and ours is the heaviest train that has left Cape Town.

February 22.—Still travelling. Arrived at De Aar at 5.15 P.M., and heard there that we were to go on to Orange River. Left again at 8, and arrived at Orange River at 2 A.M.

February 23.—We stayed in the carriages till 5 A.M. and then marched up to camp, 900 yards north-east of the station. Albemarle with the remainder of the battalion, except forty-five men and Lieutenant Alt, arrived in camp at 4 P.M. We furnish two night-picquets, total strength of two officers and forty men, on the high ground east of the camp. Called on General Settle, the commandant.

C. Company, under Captain Matthey, proceeded to Witteputs on detachment. Had an urgent order to send an officer and forty men to Wigtown to defend a railway culvert. I sent down to the station to intercept Lieutenant Alt's party, just arrived from Cape Town, and despatched them, substituting Lieutenant Green for Lieutenant Alt. Had a bathing parade. Received an order for a company to occupy Fort Munster for the night; sent out A. Company, Captain Reid.

A dust-storm broke over camp at 5 P.M., followed by a severe thunderstorm and torrents of rain, which lasted for three hours.

February 24.—At 4 A.M. an alarm took place. One of the camp guard sentries called out for the guard, and after a time it was discovered that some of our mules and horses had stampeded. The picquets and A. Company looked very weather-beaten when they marched into camp about 7 A.M.

An order came at 9 A.M. for the line taken up by A. Company last night to be occupied permanently by a company. B. Company accordingly marched out of camp at 10 A.M.

February 25.—Cancelled church parade to enable men to clean up, dry their clothes, &c.

Newton and Watson left us yesterday on their return to England. They have been on very friendly terms with all the officers, and have identified themselves in every way with the battalion.

An alarm sounded at headquarters at 7 A.M. Our men fell in very promptly, and F. Company under Captain Edis was actually on the march to its position before the remainder of the battalion had wholly fallen in. General Settle came round our positions and was pleased, but not with the range-finding of the picquets, which had not been sufficiently practised. The English mail arrived.

February 26.—Very hot.

Had usual parades, including bathing parade,

at which half the men always have to be armed in order to cover those who are in the water.

At 9 P.M. had a letter from Station Commandant ordering *me* to go with a detachment of 400 men by the 6 A.M. train to De Aar. We stayed up most of the night making arrangements.

February 27.—A., F., G., and H. Companies were the ones selected, the staff officers being Bailey, Trotter, Sleman, and Orr. We took six signallers, one machine-gun, but no cyclists, and the total of rank and file was 399. We struck tents at 4.30 A.M., and parading at 5.30, reached the station at 6 A.M. The train did not start till 8 A.M., and very hot it was for the men in open trucks. We arrived at De Aar at 2.15 P.M. and marched into camp above the cemetery. We did not get our rations (tinned) till 5.30 P.M., although I had wired from Orange River that we should want them. Dined at the Station Hotel with Orr and Maberly (R.A.).

February 28.—A. Company marched out of camp at 6.30 A.M. for Britstown, in order to join a small force under Colonel Adye. I went to the station to pay my respects to Lord Kitchener, who was passing through. He was very nice about the regiment, promised to try to get us together later, and assented to my wish to take back to Orange River the two companies not required by Adye. At my request also he wired for the battery at Cape Town and the mounted infantry at Stellenbosch to come north: altogether, a very satisfactory interview. We all dined at the railway station, walked home in a terrific sand and thunder storm, and found tents down in camp.

March 1.— G. Company marched out of camp at 6 A.M. to follow A. Company to Britstown; Bailey accompanied. The remaining two companies were to have returned to Orange River, but there was no rail transport available.

March 2.—All of us who were left at De Aar returned to Orange River, We started at 6 P.M. and arrived at 11.40 P.M., remaining in our carriages till 5.30 A.M., and then marched to camp.

March 3.—Found that D. Company had

gone on convoy duty to Witteputs. They returned at 2 P.M.

I went by train at 11 A.M. to visit C. Company at Witteputs, and was much pleased with the soldier-like appearance of their camp. They are doing their duty there well. Brown accompanied me, and we lunched with Matthey and M'Donnell, subsequently returning by train, and visiting H. Company detachment on the way, which we also found in a creditable state of watchfulness.

E. Company left to-day to camp at Orange River Bridge as a guard; F. Company, 144 strong, also marched away to Zoutpans Drift (12 miles). These two duties are thrown on us by a sudden order withdrawing the Warwick Regiment from Orange River. Triggs left to-day for Modder River in order to settle the accounts of the mounted infantry.

March 4.— Church parade at 6.30 A.M. Wired to O. C., F. Company, to send back corporal and twelve cyclists for the flying column. The Warwick Regiment left to-day, so we are responsible for all duties, including funerals, digging graves, &c.

Smith was sent off at a moment's notice to De Aar to draw stores for the column. Orr left at 6 P.M. for Cape Town, to confer with Abe Bailey about transport.

March 5.—Triggs and Smith returned early, the former not having been able to catch the mounted infantry. General Settle left with his flying column, so the command of this district, from here to Honeynest Kloof, devolves on me. He takes Lance-Corporal Fernie and twelve cyclists with him. Albemarle left for Kimberley on duty in connection with our transport. Trotter acts as chief staff officer to me. Cohen, signalling officer, who has arranged a capital line of stations for day and night work between fifty and sixty miles long, has been made district signalling officer, and is untiring in his work.

Received a cable from the Lord Mayor, announcing that Lord Roberts had accepted the Honorary Colonelcy of the regiment. All ranks are delighted at the good news.

March 6.—I had the following telegram from Lord Roberts:—" Please announce to regiment that, at request of Lord Mayor,

LINES OF COMMUNICATION

I have with very great pleasure accepted the Honorary Colonelcy of the City Imperial Volunteers." To which I replied, "The City Imperial Volunteers are much honoured and gratified by your telegram announcing that you have accepted the Honorary Colonelcy of the regiment."

March 7. — Triggs again left to try and find the mounted infantry. I heard that there had been an engagement near Britstown yesterday, but no details are to hand.

Pawle reports that fifty of our men at Zoutpans Drift had assisted some mounted infantry of the Worcesters to withdraw a farmer and £900 worth of stock from his farm. The mounted infantry were engaged with the Boers, who tried to cut off the convoy.

March 8.—Pawle reports that last night, hearing that Parkinson, the farmer, had left a large boat behind, Hole, with two men, volunteered to go and burn it. They succeeded in doing this, having a twenty-four mile march, and returned at daylight. Had a telegram from Bailey, reporting that in action near Britstown on 6th, seven men were wounded and six missing. Inundated with telegrams all day in the General's office.

Captain Seale (Cape Police) called to see me. He has had his house and everything he possesses burnt by the Boers, his wife and child just escaping in time to Grahamstown. He is very bitter against some of the traitorous magistrates: he goes on at once to join General Settle.

March 9.—Miller (E. Company) reported seriously ill with dysentery. I go and see him daily in hospital. He is despondent about himself, but I hope he will pull through. Telegram from Bailey from Britstown:— "Wounded 6th, Colour-Sergeant Taylor, Bugler Kay, Privates Dudley, Wilkinson, A. T. Saunders, Lance-Corporal Selfe, Signaller Hamilton; prisoner, Sergeant Monk; missing, Privates Henderson, Peterson, Ripson, Nollers, Humphries. Wounded all slight, doing well."

Went down to the station just before midnight to meet Lord Kitchener's special, but he was asleep and did not show.

March 10.—I received a sudden order for a

OUR MAXIMS

Photo by Capt. Orr

To face p. 38

company to proceed to Belmont, so sent D. Company with Captain Mortimore in charge, and Smith as his subaltern. They relieve a company of the Munster Fusiliers which has moved on to Klokfontein.

Went to call on 6th Battalion Lancashire Fusiliers, who arrived from England last night.

Cohen's signalling is working admirably; his "stations" are open day and night, and the total length of line is 104 miles.

Letter from Britstown shows that our losses last Tuesday were incurred through having to retire before a superior force.

March 11.—Divine service at 6.45 A.M., followed by Holy Communion. Mr. Rose, the chaplain, came from New South Wales with troops. Capital sermon on the important part which active service plays in a man's life; he spoke feelingly of how much more those are to be pitied who are left behind. English mail in in the forenoon.

During lunch I was sent for to see Miller of E. Company. I went straight to the hospital, but the poor fellow could not speak, though I think he recognised me. He died peacefully while I was there.

We had a voluntary evening service in camp at 6.45, with that lovely hymn, "At even, ere the sun was set," and one could not help looking westward at the superb sunset.

I was glad to hear to-day from Cholmondeley.

March 12.—We buried Miller this morning at 6. A simple and impressive service in the little enclosure between us and Signal Hill. Heard of the death yesterday at Cape Town of Private G. W. Cooper, mounted infantry (wounded).

A Reuter to-day announced that a baronetcy has been conferred on the Lord Mayor and knighthood on the two Sheriffs. I cabled at once, "All ranks delighted. Warmest congratulations." There is real pleasure expressed at the honour conferred on the Lord Mayor.

Mr. Parkinson, who was rescued on the 7th instant, came to return thanks. He lunched, and we had a long talk. Trotter went to Hopetown to see the magistrate about prosecuting some of the Boer prisoners.

March 13.— I started early, riding with Corporal Eaton for Zoutpans Drift, trying for a buck on the way. We saw several, but neither stalking nor driving could bring us near our quarry.

Found all well at the detachment, with every one working hard. Orr returned late from Cape Town.

March 14.—Triggs rejoined, bringing with him Captain Reid of the mounted infantry, who stayed with us till late at night, and then returned to Kimberley.

Trotter and I dined with the Lancashire Fusiliers Militia.

March 15.—Rode early to Witteputs, where I saw C. Company, under Captain Matthey, do field-firing. The practice was well gone through, though a retirement I ordered was not successful, and section commanders showed a want of initiative. The marksmanship was good.

Heard to-day of the entry of Lord Roberts into Bloemfontein, and had a telegram from there from Cholmondeley.

Dysentery still rather prevalent, but we have only two bad cases in hospital, Harden and Harridine, the latter suffering from pneumonia; both are, happily, slightly on the mend.

March 16.—Heard from Bailey to-day about the fight of the 6th, which was a hard one for our men, as, after two nights without sleep, and with hardly any food, they had to march ten miles, and at the end of it fight for eight hours. But they behaved well and earned praise.

March 17.—We tried the Maxims to-day with their new shields, and they worked well.

English mail arrived—nine huge sacks. I wrote to Lord Roberts, saying how fit the men are, and how anxious to get to the front. Lieutenant Benson proceeded to Cape Town on the 14th, to relieve Captain Cousens at the depôt. Five dismounted men of the mounted infantry arrived to-day with two truck loads of stores from Enslin. Sleman and Firth went to Kimberley on two days' leave.

March 18.—Usual church parade at 6.45 A.M. We received yesterday from the Remount Department forty American mules, which seem a useful lot.

March 19.—Sleman and Firth returned. Hole is transferred to Wigtown, Green returning thence to headquarters. Brailey (M.I.) arrived from Bloemfontein and went on to Kimberley.

March 20.—Albemarle, Burnside, Cohen, and I left by 6.20 A.M. train for Belmont. We went out thence to Richmond (12 miles), where I inspected the post, and decided to reinforce it by two guns and the company C.I.V. from Van Wyck's farm. Major Penny, commandant, and Major Bailey, his staff officer, were there to advise. We slept at Van Wyck's, where Mortimore and D. Company are stationed. Found them well and cheery. Played rounders, jingle, &c.

March 21.—We walked after breakfast to Mr. Thomas's farm, where Lord Methuen slept the night before the battle of Belmont. I saw there Blundell's grave. We then walked, driving part of the way, to the battlefield, and went up Scots Ridge—the one captured by the Scots Guards—now occupied by a signalling party of the C.I.V. The kopje taken by the Grenadiers was a desperate hill. Altogether we had a very interesting morning. There were many signs of the battle still remaining.

I signed at the Commandant's office the new orders for the O. C. troops at Richmond, and we decided to send out there twenty mounted infantry from Fincham's farm, in addition to the other reinforcements. Returned to Orange River, arriving there at 2 P.M. Found Ridler had come over from Bloemfontein.

March 22.—Cousens returned to duty with the battalion from the base. Albemarle, Orr, and I rode over to Zoutpans Drift and slept there.

March 23.—We tried for buck in the morning, the mounted infantry acting as beaters. They bagged one, but we guns were unsuccessful, although we saw several. Back in the afternoon to Orange River. English mail arrived. Very wet to-day and a cold night.

March 24.—Still wet and rather cold. Ridler (M.I.) returned to Bloemfontein with a few

WRECKED BRIDGE AT NORVAL'S PONT

Photo by Capt. Orr

To face p. 44

LINES OF COMMUNICATION

details and stores. Brailey, who was to have taken the party back, is detained here, sick.

March 25.—Again cold and boisterous weather. Usual church parade. Colonel Maxwell arrived to take over General Settle's command, but went on to Kimberley to confer with Lord Methuen. Sorry to hear by telegram that Trotter's brother (Grenadiers) was seriously wounded yesterday near Bloemfontein.

March 26.—Handed over district to Colonel Maxwell. Orr and I left by mail at 5 P.M. for Bloemfontein. Reached De Aar at 11.30 P.M. Stayed there three hours.

March 27.—Arrived at Naauwpoort at 7 A.M., where I breakfasted, and met Colonels Goldsmid, Calley, Gough, &c.

Arrived at Norval's Pont at 1. The bridge here having been blown up by the Boers, we took five hours crossing on a pontoon and getting the baggage transhipped.

March 28.—Arrived at Bloemfontein 1 A.M. and stayed in the train till 6. Breakfasted at the Bloemfontein Hotel; then went to the hospital and was glad to hear that G. Trotter is out of danger, though not yet allowed to see any one; then went to see Crabbe and Codrington (wounded), and on to the Fort, where the 2nd Battalion Coldstream Guards are quartered. At 12 o'clock we went to the Presidency, where Lord Roberts at once saw me. He told me the battery and the infantry battalion would come up and join his army. He evidently takes great interest in the C.I.V.

Then we drove out five miles to Austen's Farm, to see our mounted infantry, but were disappointed to find that they had just marched off twenty miles to the Glen, under sudden orders. However, on returning to the town, we saw Ridler, and had a talk with him. I went back in the afternoon to see Lord Roberts, who told me that there was a preference for the slouch hat over the helmet, and that we could continue ours in wear, and send the helmets into store. He also told me we could bring up our ambulance waggon, and our cyclist and signalling sections complete. He was much struck with our list of professions of the men,[1] and ordered several

See Appendix A.

copies to be struck off. Altogether my two interviews were satisfactory and very gratifying.

I saw Sir A. Milner and General Sir F. Walker, both of whom are staying here.

Afterwards we walked out to see the 9th Division, where I met Ruggles, who is very well, and we had a good talk with him. Dined at the Hotel, and got into our train at 10 P.M.

March 29, 30.—Started at 7 A.M., and, after a long delay at Norval's Pont, reached De Aar at 3.30 A.M. and left at 5.30. Ten miles out, a truck ran off the line, which delayed us, so that we did not get to Orange River till 11 A.M. Found on arrival that orders had been received for the battalion to proceed to-morrow to Norval's Pont. All the companies on detachment except A. and G. joined during the day.

Shocked to hear that Colonel Gough, who had travelled with us on Tuesday to Norval's Pont, had died suddenly soon after we parted company.

CHAPTER III

ORANGE RIVER TO THE VAAL

[LORD ROBERTS had by now moved up to the front at Modder River, and after Cronje had been captured at Paardeberg had occupied Bloemfontein. Ladysmith was relieved.]

March 31.—The battalion left in two special trains under command of self and Albemarle at 10.15 and 10.45 A.M. At De Aar the two trains were joined together.

April 1.—We arrived at Naauwpoort at 1 A.M., where we were told we should have to detrain owing to a block on the line beyond us. Detrained at 6 A.M., and marched into camp on the hill east of the station.

April 2.—Trotter left for Bloemfontein to see his brother. Brailey also left us to rejoin the mounted infantry. Albemarle and I dined with General Brabazon.

April 3.—Practised field-firing on the south side of camp; not good on the whole, the volleys being distinctly bad, and initiative on the part of section commanders being almost wholly wanting. Still all ranks enjoyed the work and did their best. Paraded at 7.15, and got back at 1.

April 4.—Again practised field-firing over the same ground, but with the order of the companies changed. A distinct improvement was shown in the volleys; but the section commanders are still weak, not seeming to grasp the importance of their commands.

Went over the large station hospital, where there are 600 sick and wounded. The arrangements are admirable, the patients being put up in marquees, nine or ten in each.

I dined with Colonel Goldsmid, and met Colonel Fairholm, the acting camp commandant.

April 5.—A telegram from Orange River announces death from enteric of Private Walker, whom we left behind very ill.

Battalion had a route march this morning. In the afternoon we fired a match at unknown ranges between F. Company and the Hampshire Yeomanry—twenty men, 30 rounds each. We won, getting a percentage of 12 to their 6.50. Albemarle and I went later to the station hospital, where our officers and men gave an entertainment for the sick and wounded patients, which was very much appreciated. Among the officers assisting were Treffry, Hole, and Marsh.

April 6.—Trotter returned early. We received this week's English mail, but last week's is still at Bloemfontein.

April 7.—We had a battalion drill this morning; the men were steady and attentive, but the N.C.O.'s are shaky in all their parade movements. We shot another match against the Hampshire Yeomanry, this time a team of C. Company representing the C.I.V. The competition was much the same as that of two days ago, except that it was at, approximately, from 1000 to 200 yards. Our percentage of hits was 43.2, and that of the Yeomanry 37. We also played a football match against the Town, which we won by one goal to none.

We are furnishing many fatigues here,

some of 100 men for R.E. works, also strong ones for Ordnance Stores, and several funeral parties.

Jeffery came into hospital here this morning from Norval's Pont with dysentery.

We were warned to-night that we might have to entrain to-morrow, but the order was subsequently cancelled. We attended church parade with the whole garrison this morning, and as the chaplain was unwell I had to officiate.

April 9.—We practised field-firing again, and on the whole there was a distinct improvement, though a flank movement was not very well carried out. Still, we have been fortunate in having the chance of these useful practices, and I am sure that we have learnt much. In the evening Trotter gave instruction in shelter trench exercise, which was much appreciated, hardly a single officer or man having ever done it before.

April 10.—At 7.45 this morning we received the order for all our baggage to be down at the station by 9 A.M., and for the battalion to entrain by 10.45 A.M. Tents were struck very smartly, and the battalion was at the station "on time." We all left together about 12 noon in open trucks, and at 10 P.M. we were ordered to turn out at Norval's Pont, where we lay on the ground near the station, and bivouacked for the night. Jeffery accompanied us. Sleman remained behind with a slight attack of dysentery.

April 11.—The 2nd Battalion Scots Guards passed through this morning, and we had an hour's talk with them; also with the Brigadier, Bar Campbell, and Gascoigne, the Brigade-major. We entrained by companies in goods trains, sitting on the tops of tarpaulins and coal-trucks, E. Company starting first under Pawle, then H. Company with self and headquarters. We detrained at Springfontein at 7 P.M., and bivouacked for the night alongside the Scots Guards.

April 12.—Edis arrived with F. Company at 3 A.M., and Albemarle with the other three companies at 6 A.M. We pitched camp in the forenoon. The Scots Guards marched off north in the afternoon. We can get no news of Bailey and A. and G. Companies.

ORANGE RIVER TO THE VAAL

Albemarle and I dined with the Militia Battalion of the Argyll and Sutherland Highlanders, and met Tom Cochrane.

April 13.—Had a parade in marching order, and fitted our entrenching picks and shovels. Glad to get a telegram from Orr that he and transport left Orange River last night. Cohen went to Bloemfontein to try and recover our lost mail.

April 14.—Orr and all his transport arrived; the animals look very fit.

April 15.—Easter Sunday. Cohen returned early with thirty-four large sacks of mails, which were a joy to all ranks. A pouring wet day, with two very heavy thunderstorms, which converted the camp into a lake. Had to cancel church parade.

Received orders to be in readiness to march to-morrow for Bloemfontein. Triggs proceeded by rail to join the mounted infantry for temporary duty. Sorry to hear that Sleman has got enteric.

April 16.—We marched off at 2 P.M., getting to Kuilfontein at 4.30 P.M. (seven miles), where we camped.

April 17.—We marched at 9 A.M., and arrived at Jagersfontein (twelve miles), where we camped. My command consists of 800 of the C.I.V., 220 Canadian Dragoons, an Army Service Corps Company, 750 loose remount horses, 1200 loose remount mules, 250 Indians and 200 natives; a mixed but an interesting force. My two mounted orderlies were a Canadian and a Sikh.

April 18.—Wet night and raining all day. We marched at 9 A.M., and took four hours to cross one drift (the column stretches for 2½ miles); therefore, as the weather was so bad, we halted at Kruger's Siding (eight miles), and camped. The 2nd Battalion Grenadiers passed in the train to-day, and we talked with some of them while the train stopped. Very heavy marching, and the men got wet through.

April 19.—We paraded at 9 A.M. and camped at Edenburg (seventeen miles): a longish march, but accomplished under perfect conditions of climate and good conditions of road, the going only being heavy in places. A great many men fell out and had to be carried in the ambulance. They complain greatly of the bandolier, as being not only a weight on the chest, but as not helping to balance the equipment, which a weight on the front part of the waist-belt, such as the old pouches were, would do. Some of the men prefer to wear the bandolier round their waists.

The Sherwood Foresters' band met us outside Edenburg, and played us into camp.

April 20.—We marched at 9 A.M. The country gets greener and prettier every day. We hear a great deal of the Boers being near us, but neither our advance nor rear guard of Canadians has seen anything. We halted at Bethanie (fourteen miles), where we found the 3rd Battalion Royal Scots, who were very hospitable to us.

April 21.—Marched sixteen miles to Kaffir River. The Cameron Highlanders are here, and some of us dined with them. We are glad to know that we are in the same brigade.

A great many men again fell out owing to the heat: this makes me rather nervous for the future. Newtown Butler and three or four officers of the Guards are here, awaiting train-transport. Cousens was overcome by heat, and has to go to Bloemfontein by train.

April 22.—Marched twelve miles to Kaal's Spruit. The sun has made the going much better. Three companies of the Derby Regiment went with us. The Canadian Dragoons went on to Bloemfontein, leaving a troop behind to go with us to-morrow. We heard firing on our flank to-day.

April 23.—Arrived in camp at Bloemfontein at 12.30 P.M. We are two miles south of the town, near the railway, on the west side. I rode to headquarters later, and called on the Commander-in-Chief and staff. Saw Crabbe and various other friends.

April 24.—A much-needed rest for the men. I went out to Sussex Hill to see A. and G. Companies, who, under Bailey, had arrived a few days previously by train.

Lord Roberts inspected the battalion at 4.30 P.M., and was pleased with the appearance and steadiness of the men. Had orders to proceed to-morrow to the Glen.

Cousens tells me that the doctors won't allow him to come to the front any more, and he fears he will have to retire from the regiment.

April 25.—The battalion marched off for the Glen at 8.40 A.M., stopping nearly an hour at the railway station for A. and G. Companies to join them. Triggs stays behind with a depôt of sick men. Ryan of the mounted infantry comes with us to take Sleman's place. We saw a good deal of Cholmondeley and the mounted infantry, and were very glad to meet them; and several of the officers rode with the battalion part of the way. I went to hospital to see Audley Neeld and Arthur O'Neill. We arrived at the Glen at 4.30 P.M. and bivouacked for the night, relieving the Norfolk Regiment.

April 26.—We pitched camp, and found a great many men for outposts and various fatigues. This is the only pretty part of South Africa I have yet seen. I appointed Orr railway staff officer. Sleman joined us unexpectedly to-night.

April 27.—We are to form part of the 21st Brigade, which assembles here. The Cameron

Highlanders, Derbyshire, and Sussex joined the camp, also the Brigadier, General Bruce Hamilton, and Major Shaw, Brigade-Major, so we are now complete. Pawle proceeds to Cape Town, to try and get up for us the men's jerseys and some more clothing. Ryan rejoins the mounted infantry.

Heard firing in the south-east. A big Boer commando reported due east.

When we met the Grenadiers the other day, one of the men put his head out of the train, and seeing our miserable plight (we were all wet through and our transport was stuck in a deep drift) said to me, "Well, sir, and how do you like the army now?" (!)

On one of the last days of our march, as Ted Trotter was walking with his head down past some of the Derbyshire Regiment, one of them was heard to say, "Don't he wish himself back at the Mansion-House!"

The following militia story was told me by the major of the regiment concerned. The countersign was "collapsed" (it had been "routed" the day before). A militiaman approached the sentry. "Halt, who comes there?" "Routed." "Shure, it's not 'routed' at all; it's 'collapsed!'"

April 28.—A detachment of our mounted infantry passed through *en route* from Karee to Bloemfontein.

April 29.—Church parade in brigade, 6.30 A.M. Received orders at 9 A.M. to march at 1. Struck camp, and sent back to Bloemfontein our tents and all our baggage, except thirty-five lbs. per officer, and greatcoat, one blanket, and one waterproof sheet per man.

The brigade marched to Kleinospruit and there bivouacked.

April 30.—Marched off at 7.30 A.M. Saw parties of Boers on Schanskraal, on the east side of us. General Tucker's division was heavily engaged to the north-east, and we could see his shells bursting. The enemy retired as we advanced. Ultimately our brigade halted on the Os Spruit, to the south of Schanskraal (seven miles).

May 1.—Reveillé at 4 A.M. We marched at 5, the C.I.V. forming the advance guard. We went through some very pretty but dangerous glens and passes, and halted at mid-day at Kaalfontein, where we found Broadwood's cavalry brigade. We continued about 2 P.M., marching parallel to the cavalry, and south of them.

About 3 P.M. we sighted the enemy on a kopje some 2500 yards to our right front. They opened fire on us, on which I sent on Loch's scouts, followed by A. and B. Companies in attack formation. The Boers retired as we advanced, and we then continued our march to a point near Jacobsrust, seeing a great many shells bursting three and four miles ahead of us. Ian Hamilton and his mounted infantry, who had had two days' fighting, bivouacked alongside of us. Our eighteen-mile march was a severe one for our men, as it lasted altogether eleven hours.

One squadron of our C.I.V. was among the mounted infantry who came in to-day, commanded by Waterlow. They had three wounded.

The men thoroughly enjoyed their tot of rum to-night, and quite deserved it, for only ten fell out during the day.

May 2.—We turned out at 4 A.M. expect-

ORANGE RIVER TO THE VAAL

ing an early start, but, to our great relief, the march was cancelled, and a day's halt ordered. The washing of our bodies and clothes was the principal occupation.

I had a long talk with Ian Hamilton, who came to our lines and asked to be introduced to all the officers. We sent three men back sick with a convoy. All ranks had a welcome ration of rum.

May 3.—Reveillé at 4.30. Marched at 6.30, and remained all day in extended order expecting to see the enemy. Heavy firing heard. Bivouacked at Isabellafontein (twelve miles).

May 4.—Marched off at 6.30. We are now incorporated with our brigade in General Ian Hamilton's division. General Sir H. Colvile's division remains from five to ten miles in rear of us.

We found the Boers holding two kopjes, one on each side of us. About five miles after we started a heavy artillery duel ensued, in which our guns made excellent practice. Our battalion lay down in a mealie field, with shells bursting over us, but fortunately no one was hurt. We then attacked (with

H. Company) a kopje to our right front. The enemy retired, and our company on gaining the top sent several volleys after them, and we could see the whole Boer force retreating at best speed. We bivouacked on the side of the Wet Spruit after a hard day and a sixteen-mile march.

May 5.—Reveillé at 5, and we marched at 7, the transport getting across the Spruit beforehand. We expected a big battle at the drift of the river Wet; but although the Boers had a great opportunity at that point, they had not taken advantage of it, and, to our surprise, we encountered no opposition.

We arrived at Winburg at 4 P.M. (fifteen miles), where, after pulling ourselves together, we marched through the town. A great many houses were shut up, though there were several people who were glad to see us. It is a very pretty, clean town. We camped a mile outside, on the north-east.

Although to-day's march was exciting, it was very hot, and the men are rather beat, but they show an admirable spirit, and no one falls out without good reason. I am

ORANGE RIVER TO THE VAAL 63

very proud of their marching, which improves daily.

May 6.—General Bruce Hamilton tells me in confidence that we shall start off again this evening, but that the move is to be kept secret. We had a restful day in camp. Colvile marched in with the Highland Brigade in the afternoon.

We moved off at 5 P.M., leaving behind us Townroe with forty-nine men unfit to march. At 9 P.M., after proceeding ten miles, we bivouacked. Three of our privates are now employed as medical officers, Rusby and Glover with the Bearer Company, and Weekes with the 300 sick the brigade leave behind, most of whom he will accompany in the convoy to Bloemfontein. The Brigadier saw these men to-day, and gave them all the temporary rank of sergeant-major. It is a record, I should say, for a regiment to be able to furnish three medical officers out of its ranks for the staff of the army.

We halted ten miles out from Winburg and bivouacked.

May 7.—A welcome day of rest, and it is a

great blessing to feel that we are now in the forefront of the army, and always camping on ground which is clean and fresh.

May 8.—Not yet moving, as we understand we have been pushing on too much. Had to send Treffry and five men back to Winburg sick—all with dysentery.

We are now killing our own meat, which enables us to issue it earlier, but it has to be cooked directly it is killed. The men prefer to have it issued raw and to cook it, each man in his own mess-tin. Their first attempts in the culinary art were amusing, several trying to roast (?) their meat over a tallow candle.

The name of the place we are now at is Dankbaarsfontein. After dinner Orr dug out (I had got leave from superior authority) a supposed grave in the Boer cemetery, which had a suspicious covering of fresh earth, but we found nothing, not even a body. It was curious, for the earth must have come from somewhere—probably the garden of the farm near by.

May 9.—Marched off at 7 A.M., and bivouacked at Bloomeplaatz—twelve miles. The

OUR WATER-CART

Photo by Capt. Orr

To face p. 64

country is prettier than any we have yet seen, with a few trees, fair water, and comfortable farmhouses.

May 10.—Reveillé at 3; marched at 4.30 A.M. to the drift on the Zand River (three miles), where the Boers are supposed to be in strength. Forded the river, about two feet deep. We were in action a great part of the day, and our brigade lost two killed and twelve wounded; two of our sergeants were hit in the hand. After a somewhat stubborn resistance, the enemy retired; we followed for three or four miles, and camped at Deelfontein Zuid. The men had thirteen hours altogether, and we must have covered eighteen miles. Orr captured a Boer prisoner directly after the action with his bandolier on, but we could not get his rifle.

We are now only three miles from Ventersberg, and the head-men tendered their submission this evening.

Corporal Fernie and his cyclists rejoined us to-night. Our present strength at headquarters is 27 officers and 845 men present for duty; 6 officers and 198 men of the infantry battalion are also in South Africa. Our total sick are 3 officers and 198 men, but the large majority of these are convalescent, and only awaiting an opportunity to return to duty.

May 11.—Marched at 12.15 P.M., but were sent in a wrong direction, and had to retrace our steps, passing our old camping-ground at 1.20 P.M. Reached our bivouac at 6.15 P.M.—a sixteen-mile march. Not a particle of wood to be had, nor a drop of water, and in many cases the meat could not be cooked! To add to the discomfort only half a ration of tea has been issued, so the night was pretty miserable.

May 12.—We formed the baggage-guard to-day for the whole division, and marched off at 9 A.M. We had a long halt in the middle of the day, and arrived at our bivouac, four miles south of Kroonstadt, at 6.30 P.M.—seventeen miles, the men being tired after two very hard days.

We have one commandant, Cairncross, and 23 men, prisoners. He is of Scottish descent, and is a very agreeable man to talk with. He explains many things which we did not understand in our last two actions, and thinks the end of the war is not far off.

ORANGE RIVER TO THE VAAL

May 13.—This is good camping-ground, but the water is bad. We had brigade church parade at 10 A.M.

Jonah, Ted, and I rode into Kroonstadt in the afternoon, and went to see the brigade of Guards, having tea with the Coldstream and then with the Grenadiers. They have done uncommonly well, and are highly spoken of on all sides. I dined with our General (Bruce Hamilton) in the evening.

Townroe and Treffry rejoined us, having made twenty-eight miles of their journey by trolley (pushed by natives) up the railway line.

May 14. — Lord Roberts inspected our brigade, and told me he was much pleased with the C.I.V. I rode into Kroonstadt in the evening, and dined with Ward, having a lovely ride back, later, in the full moonlight.

May 15.—We marched off at 9 A.M., and halted at Kransspruit Zuid (seven miles). We are the same force as we were before under Ian Hamilton. We left McDonnell and 25 men behind, footsore and otherwise unfit to march. Our mounted infantry (Waterlow's squadron) are with us in this division.

May 16.—Marched thirteen miles easterly.

May 17.—Reveillé at 4.15. Marched off at 6.15, and "nooned" for three hours on the south bank of the Valsche river. We had a succession of bad drifts to ford, and reached our halting-place at 6 o'clock, eighteen miles; but having to wait till 2 A.M. for our baggage was cold work, as the men had come in very hot, and had nothing to cover themselves with except the one blanket they carry. We did not issue all the blankets before 2.30.

May 18.—At 3 A.M. forty men drew rations, the animals being killed as the fatigue party arrived to draw the meat. Reveillé was at 4.30, so we had next to no sleep, and it was a bitterly cold night with a frost; all ranks were pretty uncomfortable. At 6.25 A.M., just as I was marching off as an advanced guard, an order came postponing the march till 7 A.M.—rather annoying when, after a great effort, we had got all ready to the minute.

It was a very hot day, the light breeze there was being behind us, and the men suffered severely. We halted for two hours to cook dinners (each man cooking his own in his mess-tin, as they always do now), and arrived at the town of Lindley at 5 P.M. We bivouacked half a mile west of it. Twenty-seven men fell out during the march, and this was not at all a large number, considering what we had gone through.

Directly we arrived in camp we had to send out two and a half companies on all-night outpost duty, and forty men went into town on wood fatigue. Those who were not on duty were asleep before 8 P.M.

We have seen some big veldt fires lately, and at night-time they look grand, often covering a front of over a mile. The sun sets now at 5.14 P.M., which practically gives us the shortest days of the year, so far as the evenings are concerned, though its rising, which is now at 6.30, continues to get later and later for five weeks longer. The nights are bitterly cold, with frost, and sometimes a piercing wind, and the days are hotter than they were farther south. We have had no rain at all since 18th April, and none is now due, we are told, till October.

May 19.—A very welcome day's rest, employed in washing, disinfecting water-bottles, mending waggons and harness, &c. Most of the officers went into Lindley.

May 20.—Townroe was reported unfit, and we had to leave him behind to go south with a sick convoy. Reveillé at 5, and marched off at 7. We kept on pretty steadily till 5.30, when we bivouacked at Koroospruit (sixteen miles). Our baggage, unfortunately, could only come as far as the west side of the Spruit, and it was a difficult job to get our blankets and camp-kettles. The men were tired, having had hardly any food for twelve hours.

We heard that as soon as we had left Lindley the Boers entered the town, driving out the mounted infantry, killing 7 and taking 70 prisoners. We also came across about 1500 Boers, and I extended two companies for attack, but beyond the exchange of a few shells between our artillery and theirs, nothing took place. A convoy which they had with them, containing £50,000 and a large quantity of ammunition, got away.

May 21.—Reveillé at 5, marched at 7, the C.I.V. being advance guard. The staff took

CROSSING RHENOSTER RIVER

Photo by Major Pawle

ORANGE RIVER TO THE VAAL 71

us on a wrong road, and we went at least three miles out of our way. We halted to draw biscuits at 10 A.M., otherwise we had no long halt till we got to our bivouac, two miles north of Veshkop, at 5.30. This was again a very trying day. The distance was eighteen miles, and the men had nothing for breakfast except coffee. They were consequently twenty-four hours without food. Directly we got in we had to find outposts.

May 22.—Marched at 7.15 A.M., after a cold night and the heaviest dew we have yet had. We encountered the Boers outside the town of Heilbron, but they were driven back by our artillery and mounted infantry, and we bivouacked in the outskirts of the town at 1 P.M. Twelve miles to-day, which makes a total of 102 since Kroonstad, and of 368 since we started from Springfontein.

May 23.—After various orders we marched off at 8.45 A.M., proceeding through the town, and then in a north-westerly direction.

There is nothing of interest in Heilbron except a pretty Dutch church. We managed to pick up certain stores, and it was amusing to see the miscellaneous articles which officers got for their men—sago, oatmeal, Eno's fruit salt, &c. Nothing edible or potable came amiss, for we have been almost on starvation rations.

We arrived at our bivouacking ground, Spitzkop (twelve miles), at 2 P.M. We are on rather high ground, and the weather is quite cold by day, owing to a strongish wind, generally from the east.

May 24.—The Camerons' band commenced the day with "God save the Queen," which all ranks cheered loudly. The battalion is part of the rear-guard, which also comprises the 81st field battery, 600 mounted infantry, and a section of "Pompoms," the whole of this force being under my command.

We started at 9.30 A.M., and were soon attacked by 800 Boers, whom our mounted infantry, who formed our rear screen, engaged. Three of our companies were extended; but alas! they had no chance, for, on our battery opening fire at 4400 yards, the enemy retired, and the rear-guard were not again disturbed.

ORANGE RIVER TO THE VAAL

We reached our bivouac (thirteen miles), which was east of the railway and about four miles north of Vredepoort, at 3.30 P.M. Our casualties were two men and four horses wounded.

May 25.—We saw Lord Roberts' column last night to the south, and this morning it was near us in column of route. We paraded at 7, and marched soon after; but there was much delay, partly caused by our being in mass of double company columns—a most unwieldy formation in which to pass obstacles. The Guards brigade passed us, marching by the line of railway. We ultimately halted just before dark at a point nine miles north of our last camp—an unsatisfactory day.

Now that we are headed north the men are very cheery; but their health is a good deal strained by the food—short rations of coffee and no biscuit for three days, only flour, which, in inexperienced hands, is not likely to make very nutritious food! One and a half pounds of meat are, however, issued, and if this could only be killed a reasonable time before cooking, it would be excellent. We sighted the Transvaal to-day, seeing the high hills to the north of the Vaal.

CHAPTER IV

FIGHT AT DOORN KOP

[THE army under Lord Roberts has been marching up north in several parallel columns. We, still in the 21st Brigade under Bruce Hamilton, have crossed the railway and are now on the left of the Guards brigade.]

May 26.—We marched at 7, but had to halt continually. We sighted the Vaal river about 2 P.M., and, marching along the east side of the re-entering angle, crossed it beyond Boschbank, at Wonderwater Drift. The drift was eighteen inches deep and very rocky, and the men's feet suffered as they crossed barefooted. When coming down to the drift, one native driver and four mules were killed by an accident.

We set foot on Transvaal soil about 5 o'clock, which pleased the battalion very much,

FIGHT AT DOORN KOP

and proceeded to our bivouac, some three-quarters of a mile north-west, at Driefontein. Our distance was thirteen miles.

May 27.—Marched at 8.30 north-easterly for seventeen miles, and bivouacked at Wildebeestfontein.

May 28.—The coldest night we have had, and my blanket was quite white at reveillé, which was at 4.30. The water, too, was frozen, which gives one an excuse for not washing, for it is impossible to wash even one's hands in the dark when there are four degrees of frost. We marched at 6.45, and halted north of Syperfontein (ten miles) at noon, when we heard French engaged with artillery and pom-poms to the north-west.

May 29.—Reveillé at 4.15. The battalion was advance guard to the division, and we marched off at 6.30. The guiding by the staff was very erratic, and as frequent change of direction was given, we went considerably out of our way.

At 11.45 I had an order to form up the brigade with the 76th field battery on Doornkop (the hill where Jameson surrendered).

This I did, and General B. Hamilton then came up, and explained his plan of attack to commanding officers. We were ordered to advance in attack formation from the S.W. corner of the hill in a N.W. direction across the open; to engage the enemy if found (they were believed to be in rear of a ridge 2000 yards in front), and, if not opposed, to continue our advance in the direction of Florida, a suburb of Johannesburg, and at the same time to keep touch with the 19th Brigade on our right.

I accordingly advanced the battalion at 12.40 P.M. H. Company was in front, followed by A., and the remainder in succession. There was no opposition to speak of in our immediate front, though shells were landed close to us directly we started, one of which passed over our heads and killed a Cameron sergeant in the rear. After marching about 1000 yards we came under the fire of pompoms which enfiladed us from a kopje 2500 yards on our left, and under a heavy musketry fire which enfiladed us from a kopje about 1800 yards on our right. I deemed

FIGHT AT DOORN KOP

it best to halt temporarily, as we could not return the fire on either flank, and I notified the General accordingly. Advantage was taken of every diminution of the enemy's fire to advance bit by bit, and I prolonged my line to the right for the double purpose of engaging the enemy in that quarter, and of endeavouring to get in touch with the 19th Brigade. The Maxim gun I also now got into action on the right flank. This brought down the enemy's fire so heavily that I formed the right company to the right (this was G. Company, and very well they did it under a heavy fire), and prolonged that line by still another company; both then became hotly engaged with the enemy.

On the left the firing line was steadily advancing. At 4.15 I received an order not to advance farther towards the black hill on the west; but, by the time I got to the left of the line, the company in front, which had been much impeded by the heavy pom-pom fire from that kopje, had gallantly rushed it, led by Captain Trotter, and had captured it. The company was composed of portions of A. and H. On my own responsibility, therefore, I continued the advance of two other companies in support of the one on the kopje, and moved F., the remaining company, to the right, towards a large clump of trees to the north, at once reporting my action. G. Company about this time, assisted by a section of H. Company, had got nearer to the kopje on the right, and, charging, took possession of it. By this time the sun had gone down and the fight came to an end.

I was thoroughly satisfied with the steadiness of our ranks, their disregard of danger, and the alacrity with which they obeyed orders, especially those to advance, and I feel very proud of the battalion. This is an interesting day for the English volunteer force, as it is the first occasion on which so many of them have been in any important action.

Where all behaved so well, it is invidious to say too much about individual companies or individual officers; but I must once more allude to the dash of A. and H. Companies on the left, and to the great use Captain

FIGHT AT DOORN KOP

Trotter was in leading them on to the kopje, which he did with great gallantry.

The machine-gun was very well served, and Sergeant Stevens displayed especial coolness in firing it. All the cyclists and signallers were with the battalion, and Private Fitzclarence, of the cyclists, showed special bravery in following Captain Trotter up the kopje.

Our casualties were 1 officer (Captain Berkeley) and 11 men wounded, one of them (Waterhouse) dangerously in the head, and the others for the most part slightly. Berkeley was hit in the mouth, but, although it will disfigure him, I hope and think it is not serious. I am thankful the list is so slight, for the whole battalion was under fire, and the firing line, which altogether contained 200 men, was under heavy fire for two hours.

This happy result is in great measure attributable to the intelligent manner in which the men had learnt to take cover. Captain Bailey had been indefatigable in impressing the importance of this upon them. When one saw the bullets skipping through, and in front of, and behind the ranks, one thought that not a man could escape being hit.

The enemy's loss must have been heavy, but as they usually carry away their dead and wounded, it was impossible to know the extent of it. Near the kopje on the left which we captured we found three Boers killed by our fire. We were informed by a wounded Boer whom we picked up, that two of them were the bodies of a Commandant Steynkamp, and of a Field-Cornet, respectively. The wounded Boer and two of the dead bodies were handed over to our cavalry; the other body was buried, and no identification was possible.

The number of rounds expended by the battalion was 9500, and as our fire was careful and deliberate, I can't help thinking we inflicted considerable loss on the enemy.

I accompanied the rear companies of the left half battalion to the captured kopje, at once reporting to the Brigadier that I should hold it all night unless I heard to the con-

FIGHT AT DOORN KOP

trary. Major Pawle and Bailey were there, and we all passed a miserable night. We could not light fires and I had no blanket or coat, and no food. I put on a thin rug taken from a dead Boer, and with it covered myself as well as I could.

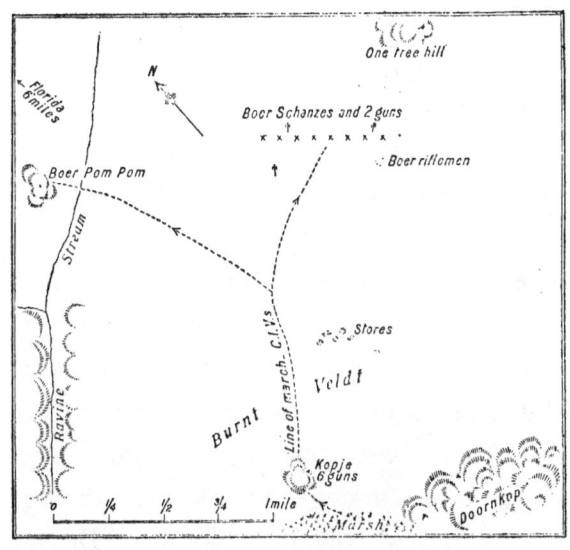

BATTLE OF DOORN KOP

CHAPTER V

DOORN KOP TO PRETORIA

[General advance of Lord Roberts' army.]

May 30.—We posted double sentries all round the kopje, and at 5 A.M. stood to arms. All was clear round us, and at 6 A.M. we started for One-Tree Hill, in reply to a summons from the Brigadier; this was four miles from our captured kopje. On arrival, we found the remainder of the battalion had marched off, and we came up with it within half a mile, but it soon proceeded on its way, and we stayed behind to get our breakfast.

We then became baggage-guard, and escorted the baggage to Florida, about six miles, where we bivouacked. Our Brigadier came into camp, and told us that General Ian Hamilton was much pleased with the behaviour of the battalion.

All ranks, although much rejoiced at the success of our fight, are completely worn out, and they thoroughly deserve a rest. Besides the fight yesterday we marched fully eighteen miles. We are in sight of Johannesburg, and at about the same level, 5600 feet. We have completed 470 miles in thirty-six marching days.

May 31.—Such a night last night—undisturbed, well-earned rest, and the sun was, for a wonder, up before several of us had been roused.

The following order was issued by our Brigadier last Saturday:—"The G.O.C. wishes to express his appreciation of the fine spirit and excellent marching shown by the troops composing the 21st Brigade. The effect of this long and rapid marching has been that the enemy has been unable to complete his preparations for defence, and has been repeatedly compelled to retire in front of us after a weak resistance."

A grand washing of men and shirts to-day in a dam near by.

I had a general parade at 5 P.M., and gave

the battalion a message of congratulation from General Ian Hamilton, and I also read the following extract from a letter sent to that General to-day by Lord Roberts:—" I am delighted at your successes, and grieved beyond measure at your poor fellows being without their proper rations. A (waggon) trainful shall go to you to-day. I expect Johannesburg to surrender this morning, and we shall then march into the town. I wish your column —which has done so much to gain possession of it—could be with us."

All our wounded are doing well; I went to see them. Poor Waterhouse was unconscious, and was about to undergo trephining.

June 1.—Marched at 12.30 to Braamfontein (eight miles), which is four miles northwest of Johannesburg. One officer per company was allowed in the town.

June 2.—Our mails arrived—three weeks' accumulation. M'Donnell also rejoined us with a dozen casuals, and brought certain stores, including the men's second pair of boots. Ten per cent. of each company had leave to go into Johannesburg.

I was busy all day with official letters, of which I had nearly two hundred, though many of these were merely vouchers for the issue of various stores.

June 3.—Marched early to Juckshai River, where we bivouacked at Deepsluit.

A great feature to-day was our passing through a wood. It really was more of an avenue than a wood, but it was quite a novelty to pass under trees at all, and they were the first we had come across in any number during 500 miles! Our bivouac, too, was close to a Spruit, with a wood alongside, so we were spared the usual painful sight of the dead-beat men toiling long distances for fuel. We covered fourteen miles to-day —quite enough, as after our halt men were hardly in their usual marching trim. A rest is essential now and again for the feet, but it is not an unmixed blessing for the stomach!

June 4.—Reveillé at 4.15. Marched at 6.15 to Hennops, or Zesmyl, Spruit. As we crossed it we heard heavy firing on the range of hills in front, a commando from Mafeking having come unexpectedly in contact with our advance guard. We were hurried up to the foot of the hills, where we lay down in reserve, and where Private A. C. Thurlow was wounded slightly. At dusk we fell back towards the Spruit and bivouacked. Distance, fifteen miles.

June 5.—An eventful day. We marched at 7, leaving four companies behind us as rear-guard under Albemarle. Every one's spirits are very high at prospect of seeing Pretoria. Our march was much impeded by every regiment wishing, apparently, to be the first in. At 9.30, on ascending some high ground, the city burst upon our view, and I must say it was an impressive moment. We marched on to our bivouac, a mile short of the racecourse, and arrived there at 12.45, the actual distance being only seven miles. We at once received orders to parade for a march through the town at 1.45, which was subsequently changed to 2.45.

We turned out as strong as possible, and the battalion, which looked very serviceable, marched past Lord Roberts in the big square in the middle of the town, the ground being kept by the Guards Brigade. We then passed through the principal streets, and as we were getting to the outskirts, Colonel Ward came up and said, "I congratulate you; the feature of the march past was the C.I.V."

To my horror we had orders to-night to move again to-morrow. I really had hoped to give the men at least a week's rest here. They are completely done up, and it was a supreme effort on the part of many of them to reach Pretoria. They are footsore and "stale," their clothes are in rags, and, for other reasons also, are quite unfit to wear, and it is impossible to get up the new clothing which we know is in South Africa for us, as the railway is not open, and we have marched far more quickly than bullock convoys.

I issued the following order to-night:—

"In congratulating the battalion on the splendid march they have made, which commenced at Springfontein on Easter Monday, 16th April, and terminated in the creditable and soldier-like parade before the Field Marshal Commander-in-Chief in Pretoria yesterday, the

Commandant publishes for information the following figures :—The march has lasted for fifty-one days ; forty of which have been marching days, the distance covered was 523 miles, which gives an average of over 13 miles per marching day."

CHAPTER VI

ROUND PRETORIA

[LORD ROBERTS' army is now in military occupation of Pretoria and the surrounding forts.]

June 6.—Trotter, Orr, and I rode over to General Smith-Dorrien's. He had asked to see me, and was now good enough to show me his despatch on our battle of 29th ultimo, in which he commanded the infantry. I give an extract, which was very gratifying: "The features of the day were the attacks of the Gordon Highlanders and the C.I.V. That of the C.I.V. convinced me that this corps at any rate of our volunteers is as skilled as the most skilful of our regulars at skirmishing.

"The men were handled with the most consummate skill by Colonel MacKinnon, Colonel Lord Albemarle, and their other officers, and it was entirely due to this skill and the quickness and dash of their movements, and taking advantage of every fold of the ground, that, in spite of a terrific fire from several directions, they drove the enemy from every position with comparatively small loss. So ended a hard day's work, an eighteen-mile march concluding with four hours' continuous fighting." We had a good talk, and renewed an acquaintance which began at Harrow in the sixties.

We then went into Pretoria, and I saw, firstly, Lord Roberts, who was very kind about the C.I.V., and with whom I had ten minutes' talk. Then I saw various staff officers with whom I had business, and we had lunch at the Grand Hotel.

We rode out at sunset to catch up the battalion, which had gone to Irene—a fourteen-mile march, lost our way on the veldt, although we kept company with a convoy, and, after much wandering about, did not get into camp till 9.30 P.M. There is something very fascinating in riding on the veldt by moonlight, especially when there is a large party of mounted men—a lot of weird figures moving along in utter silence, which is only broken by a trooper occasionally cursing a stumbling horse, and once and again by a rifle-shot as some poor worn-out animal is put out of his misery.

June 7.—Forty men "went sick" this morning, so we sent by rail thirty of the footsore ones to form an escort which we were ordered to furnish. Croft was in charge.

Matthey went off south to try to find our clothing at Bloemfontein or elsewhere. Sergeant Cheshire and twenty-nine sick men rejoined from the south.

I discharged from the service, at their own request, three cyclists, Hichens, Curtis, and Balfour. These men had important business awaiting them at home, and I obtained special leave yesterday from Lord Roberts to let them go.

This was a day of rest, which would have been more beneficial if the men could have had biscuit, but they have a ration of that horrible Boer meal instead, which is sour stuff, full of millet, impossible to bake, and induces dysentery. I had the battalion out in the afternoon, to show the shirts washed; and I spoke some words of encouragement, telling them how much their achievements in marching and fighting were appreciated by Lord Roberts. Poor chaps! they look pretty bad, and it is too hard that they can't have a good rest.

I drew £1000 from the army paymaster to-day, Albemarle kindly going into Pretoria to bring it out in gold.

June 8.—We marched eight miles north-east to Garsfontein. We were to have gone south-east, but it was changed at the last moment. Ian Hamilton's force now consists of Broadwood's Cavalry Brigade, two 5-inch guns, three batteries of artillery, four corps of mounted infantry, and our old 21st Brigade. The 19th Brigade has left us to guard the railway.

We hear officially to-night that the Field-Marshal commanding and General Botha are to confer together to-morrow regarding the capitulation of the Boer forces, and an armistice is ordered.

We have now marched 545 miles in fifty-four days, of which forty-one have been marching days, an average of thirteen and a third miles a day.

June 9.—A blessed day of rest.

ROUND PRETORIA

June 10.—Another day of rest. Albemarle took the men to church parade.

June 11.—Reveillé at 4, and marched at 6.5 south-easterly. We passed the cavalry camp, five miles off, and were then ordered to accompany the 5-inch guns. We subsequently crossed the Pienaars River, and changed our direction to the west, at once extending for attack, near Boshkop farm, G. and H. Companies being in the firing and supporting lines.

The whole battalion advanced in extended order across an open piece of ground under shell and musketry fire, gaining cover under a kopje at the end of it. G. Company was ordered to the right to take up a line of outposts which had been held by the mounted infantry, and the remainder of the battalion moved also to the right, to be in rear of the outpost line. G. kept up a smart fire on the enemy's rear-guard, who gradually retired towards the main position. H. then advanced on the right of G., finding the kopje in front of them deserted, and went through a wood in rear of it, which was also deserted, except by a Boer boy of fourteen, who had been shot through the head, and his father, who had remained behind to look after him. A native —a Swazi — was also captured, completely equipped with bandolier, &c.

It was now dusk, and the enemy had retired to the main position, which looks a most formidable place to attack to-morrow. The battalion was withdrawn to the drift which we had crossed earlier in the day, A. Company being left to relieve G. and H. on their line of outposts. Our casualties were one man (Walters, G. Company) dangerously wounded Little (C. Company) and Joliffe (D. Company), severely, and 4 men slightly.

CHAPTER VII

DIAMOND HILL

[As the Boers were known to be holding strong positions to the south-east of Pretoria, General Ian Hamilton's force was sent out to drive them back.]

June 12.—Reveillé at 4; marched at 6 back to the kopje where we had left A. Company on outpost duty. We were now facing the Boer position, which, as I said before, looks very formidable. The ascent to it is in places nearly perpendicular, and the cliffs are 200 feet high. We could see many men hurrying to and fro on the top, placing guns in position, and so on. It was a heavenly morning, perfectly still, with the clearest possible atmosphere for "spying," and the apparent peacefulness of the scene was in strange contrast with the preparations both sides were making for killing as many of their enemies as possible.

The name of our kopje is Donkerhoek, and the enemy's position is Diamond Hill, running from above Kleinfontein farm for some three miles in a south-easterly direction. Soon after eight, Reid saw a gun being placed in position on our left front, and Major Conolly, 82nd field battery, was directed to open fire on it. So at 8.45 A.M. the quiet morning was rudely disturbed by the first gun. This shelling, which was not replied to, went on for an hour or more. At 9.50 I was ordered to advance the battalion to the wood which H. Company had explored last night, and to await orders to advance.

General Bruce Hamilton explained to commanding officers that he intended to attack the big hill, the Sussex advancing on the left of the farm, the C.I.V.'s in the centre, and the Derbys on the right (the Camerons had been kept four miles in the rear). We gained the wood without being fired on, and the men cooked and ate their dinners.

At 12.40, the order came to advance, and at 12.50, twenty men of A. Company advanced, commanded by Jeffery, and preceded by four

IN CAMP

DIAMOND HILL. FIRST DAY

Photo by Major Pawle
DIAMOND HILL. THE ARTILLERY GOING INTO ACTION

To face p. 96

scouts, who, accompanied by Trotter (who had gone unknown to me), moved across the open and began the ascent. It is no exaggeration to say that the journey of these men was watched with breathless interest by the whole division. To our surprise, they gained the summit at 1.10 without being fired on, and I quickly pushed on successive lines of reinforcements, which presently came in for a good deal of fire while crossing the intervening valley. Almost our only casualty, however, here, was a mule in the machine-gun, which was disabled by a shot in the leg.

At 1.15 desultory firing began on the summit, which soon showed us that the enemy had preferred some position unknown to us farther to the rear, to opposing us on the hill-top. When I reached the summit, I found that the fire proceeded from a hill of exceptional strength, called the Black Kopje (because all the grass on the face of it was burnt), some 1500 yards north of the edge of the cliff; I also found that A. Company was prolonged to its right by H., the whole of these companies being more or less in the firing line, which was about 100 yards from the top, under a moderate cover of stones. Subsequently, Reid, with the General's acquiescence, advanced the firing line over the ridge into the open, when the men were at once exposed, and the firing became much heavier.

The remainder of the battalion stayed in the gully by which we had ascended the hill, and were under heavy dropping fire from guns and musketry. Our Maxim soon arrived on the top, being man-hauled with great difficulty by Sergeant Stevens and a fatigue party, and it was gallantly served till it was compelled to cease fire, owing to its drawing so much of the enemy's shell fire on the advance companies.

On Reid's advance, I ordered B. Company, under Green, to move up to the ridge. At 3.30 the 1st Battalion Coldstream Guards arrived, and extended on our right, but could not advance owing to the heavy fire. About this time poor Alt was wounded in the forearm, and retired a few yards to have his wound dressed. He at once tried to return

DIAMOND HILL. PART OF THE BOER FINAL POSITION FROM WITHIN

Photo by Major Pawle

to his post, but alas! a bullet hit him in the temple, and he was instantaneously killed. Several other casualties also occurred, and the wounded were gallantly looked after by Sleman and his stretcher-bearers, who were continuously exposed to terrific fire.

About 4, the 82nd field battery came into action on our extreme left, and much relieved the heavy fire under which we had so long suffered. The General, with whom I had been a great part of the afternoon, now asked me to strengthen the firing line in case he should order an assault; and so I ordered B. Company up, and found, later on, that one section of C. had also joined the firing line. Soon after, a perfect storm of musketry was kept up for two or three minutes, followed by an almost sudden cessation, although the firing was not entirely discontinued till after dark.

I relieved A. and H. Companies by B. and C., who were to remain on outpost duty, and, after slowly assembling the battalion, we marched to our bivouac at Botha's farm. The sad work of collecting the list of casualties followed, and we found that, besides poor Alt, Private Ives, D. Company, was dead, four men were severely wounded, and thirteen slightly. Poor Alt is a very great loss, for he was immensely liked in the battalion. Still an Oxford undergraduate, he was not yet in his prime, and he was more intelligent and much better informed than most.

Albemarle remained on the hill with our outposts, and sent down word late of some patrol duty of Green's, which went to prove that the Boers had evacuated their position.

I must mention the gallant conduct of Sergeant-Major Smith and Armourer-Sergeant Gordon, who, in the face of that hail of shot and bullets, took ammunition up to the front line. From beginning to end of these two days' fighting the battalion has behaved magnificently, and all ranks deserve the greatest possible credit, especially A. and H. Company to-day, who were exposed in the open for three hours to a very heavy fire.

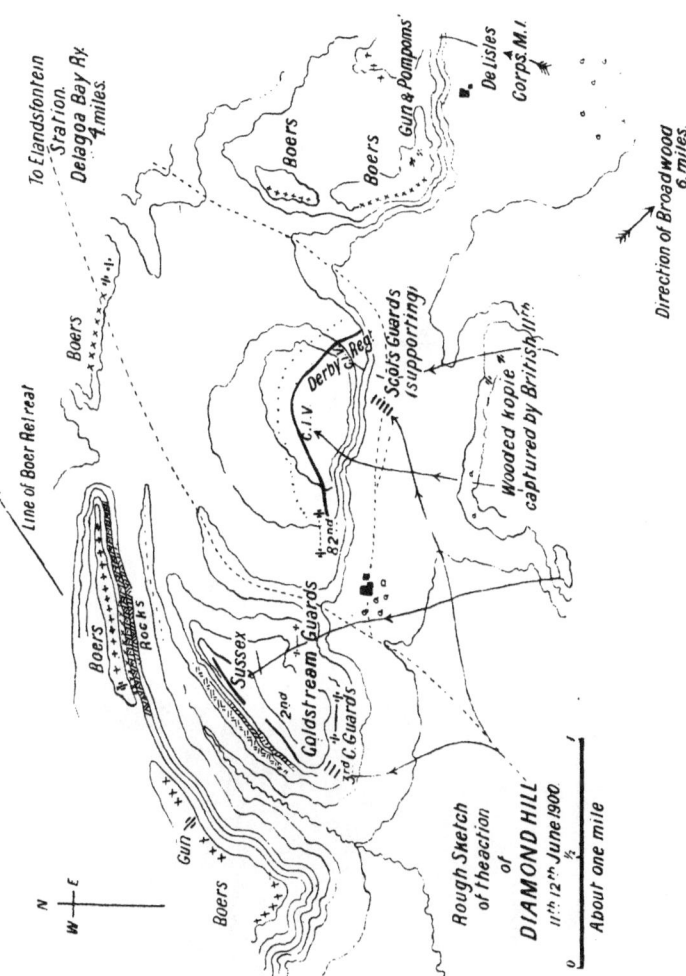

CHAPTER VIII

BACK TO PRETORIA

[THE Boers having been driven back along the Komati-Poort railway, General Ian Hamilton's force was ordered back to Pretoria.]

June 13.—We buried Alt and Private Ives at 5.40 A.M. under Diamond Hill. The funeral was most impressive from its extreme simplicity. Bailey placed the two companies concerned near the grave; the bodies were carried up on stretchers, and by the light of the full moon and of lanterns I read the last part of the burial service. The graves are about 300 yards above the farmhouse.

The battalion furnished the advance guard of four companies which marched off in a south-easterly direction along the base of the hill at 7, and the remaining four companies formed the baggage-guard under Albemarle.

I saw the wounded in hospital, who were all doing wonderfully well, and sent a cable to London. We found the Boers had retired, and we marched to Elands River, where we bivouacked. The mounted infantry were in contact with the retreating Boers to-day, and the 5-inch guns exchanged shots.

General Ian Hamilton came round and told the officers how delighted he was with the behaviour of the battalion, and said, "With such troops I could go anywhere and do anything." He also issued the following order:—"The general officer commanding Hamilton's force congratulates the troops under his command on the fine work performed by them during the past two days, which has resulted in the capture of a position of very exceptional strength, and in the flight of the enemy from the neighbourhood of Pretoria."

June 14.—Reveillé at 4, and paraded for the march at 6.15. We were to have gone twelve miles towards Pretoria, but at 6.20 the move was cancelled, and we lay in our bivouacs all day, I might almost say, lay in

BACK TO PRETORIA

our beds, for during these welcome halts officers and men never leave camp, but revel in a lazy day. We don't breakfast till 7.30; we have a great washing of bodies and linen, only half dress, eat as much as we can get, and are all in our blankets by 9 P.M.

There was some firing in the direction of Bronkhorst Spruit between the Boers and our mounted infantry, and a few shots were exchanged between the big 5-inch guns, that of the enemy being mounted on a truck on the railway line. Our mounted infantry are lying alongside of us.

June 15.—Our information being that we should probably stay here to-day, I organised an officer's party, principally of those who were engaged in the firing line, to ride over our Tuesday's battlefield on Diamond Hill.

I went, first of all, to Botha's farm to visit our wounded, four of whom I was sorry to find are in a bad way, and three of these I saw—Corporal Frapwell, who got a bullet in the left shoulder blade, which travelled down inside his body, and through the middle of it to the right side of the groin, where it now rests, and whose escape from death is a marvel; Private Eatley, who has five wounds, one in the head, one in the chest, out of which the doctor extracted a fragment of pompom two inches long, two middle fingers of his left hand smashed (they will have to be amputated), his right arm broken and his right hand crushed, the arm will have to come off; all these wounds were probably caused by one pompom shell; and Tunbridge, who was dangerously hit in the head. All our cases were being lifted into ambulances for conveyance to Pretoria.

I then went to poor Alt's grave, on which, as well as on Ives', I placed some wild flowers. Everything possible had been done to make the graves look nice, and the names, &c., had been written over the headstones.

I then rejoined the rest of the party on the top of the kopje, and most interesting it was to go over the scene of our stubborn fight. On the Black Kopje, which had been the principal part of the Boer defence, we were amazed to find how strong the position was.

From it to our front, where A. and H. Companies were, is an open bit of ground without a particle of cover, the distance being some 1500 to 2000 yards, sloping gently downwards from us for 200 or 300 yards, then flat, marshy ground, and the last 500 yards a slight ascent towards the enemy. In the position itself every single Boer had been snugly enclosed in his own little castle of rock, with parapet to fire over. The place was strewn with empty cartridge cases, no man having fired less than 100, and several of them 200.

The General estimates the enemy at 4000 strong, and as we were a third part of the infantry engaged at which they were firing, some idea may be formed of the amount of lead intended for the C.I.V. which crossed that valley. The one thing that surprised us most was why they ever gave up such a position.

On returning towards camp, we found our army had left, and we rejoined it by inclining to the west. We marched twelve miles in the direction of Pretoria, and halted at 4.30 at Schwartzkop, three miles south of Erste Fabriken Station, and close to the house of a man called Marks, a millionaire mine owner, and reputed great friend of Kruger's. Stricter orders than usual are issued as to the protection of his house (although, to the credit of our General, he does not take up his abode there, which no doubt Marks would be proud for him to do); but a feeling *will* sometimes arise that we are too considerate toward the not-wholly-civilised people we are fighting, and that if Marks and some of his millionaire confederates were made to feel some of the misery of war, this campaign would not drag on as it does. Without in any way thinking that the authorities would countenance mere consideration being shown to Marks because he is a rich man, certain it is that farmers have been more "commandeered" than he has been.

The nights are very cold now, although the sun has still great power in the daytime.

June 16.—We received orders at 11 A.M. to march at 12.30 "for Pretoria." We arrived at our camp on the east side of the town, about two miles from the middle of it, at five o'clock (thirteen miles). I dined with Pole Carew and Ruggles.

CHAPTER IX

TO HEIDELBERG

[GENERAL IAN HAMILTON was ordered to march to Heidelberg, an important station on the Natal Railway. Buller was clearing Northern Natal. De Wet very active in the Orange River Colony, breaking up the line of railway.]

June 17.—Arnold and I breakfasted with Inigo Jones. Church parade at 9.30 A.M.

All the officers lunched at the Transvaal Hotel. I went to the hospital afterwards to see our men, and was sorry to find two bad cases of enteric—Tattershall and Cheer. The wounded, except Eatley, are doing fairly well. Heavy rain this evening. Arnold and I dined with Joe Maude. I arranged to-day with Ward that Browne should be employed by the Revenue Department, in which he deserves to have a good place.

The following is an extract from Lord Roberts' army orders of 7th instant :—" The column under General Ian Hamilton marched 400 miles in forty-five days, including ten days' halt. It was engaged with the enemy twenty-eight times.

"The newly-raised battalion of the City of London Imperial Volunteers marched 500 miles in fifty-one days, only once having two consecutive days' halt. It took part in twenty-six engagements with the enemy.

"During the recent operations, the sudden variations in temperature between the warm sun in the daytime and the bitter cold at night have been peculiarly trying to the troops, and owing to the necessity for rapid movement, the soldiers have frequently had to bivouac after long and trying marches without firewood and with scanty rations. The cheerful spirit in which difficulties have been overcome and hardships disregarded are deserving of the highest praise, and in thanking all ranks for their successful efforts to attain the object in view, Lord Roberts is proud to think that the soldiers under his command have worthily upheld the traditions of Her Majesty's army in fighting, in marching, and in the admirable discipline which has been maintained throughout a period of no ordinary trial and difficulty."

June 18.—I bought 71 pairs of white moleskin trousers and 300 shirts, which were issued to the men, who had at once to burn the garments which they were intended to replace.

Sorry to find that Cheer and Eatley are both dead; they are to be buried this evening.

Ted and I lunched with Abe Bailey at the Club.

About 120 men volunteer for civil employment under the Government in South Africa, and I went over all their names with General Maxwell, Governor of Pretoria. Saw Baden-Powell as he rode into the town from Mafeking accompanied by Lord Roberts. I had no dinner, as I had to correct the list of men for employment. Walked out to camp with Orr, &c., at 9 P.M.

June 19.—The battalion on the march again, leaving at 7.30 A.M. and marching in fours past Lord Roberts near Government House. Ted and I returned afterwards to the town, where

I had much business with Ward, Cowan, Duff, and General Maxwell.

Commissions in the C.I.V. are given to Private Greenwell *vice* Grindle, retired on account of ill-health, and to Lance-Corporal Tyrwhitt *vice* Alt, killed in action. Greenwell is posted to F. Company and Tyrwhitt to H. Browne stayed behind, and we are all sorry to lose him.

Ted and I lunched with Winston Churchill, and drawing 1145 sovereigns out of the bank, sent them out in charge of eight cyclists, subsequently riding out ourselves to our camp, one and a half miles beyond Irene (fourteen miles). I found there a telegram from the Military Secretary asking if we could provide a lawyer to prosecute for the Crown at Johannesburg, and if so, to send him at once. The man was found in Private Mosley, cyclist, who started within a few minutes, and I telegraphed to Military Secretary, "Barrister despatched."

I had to leave my old bay horse behind to-day, as he is pretty well done up; I got a remount in exchange. We found Croft at

Irene; he and the party we left there had never been away.

I hope I got prospect of civil employment for several officers and men to-day, including Pawle and Marsh, but they are not to leave us till they are sent for.

It is very disappointing that the men don't have a longer rest; they require and deserve at least a week, and I told Colonel Cowan, the Military Secretary, so, as we marched into Pretoria on Saturday night.

June 20.—The battalion found advance and rear guards to-day. We marched south to Rietfontein, fifteen miles. We have the same troops with us as before, and are still called Hamilton's force.

Pom MacDonnell and I dined with Cholmondeley, who, with Waterlow's company of mounted infantry, is attached to our brigade. Rain fell to-night.

June 21.—We marched at 7.30 to Springs (fifteen miles). On the way a thunderstorm burst, accompanied by terrific hail. Some of the stones were as large as bantams' eggs, and hurt the face and hands so much that I had to halt, and turn the men's backs to the storm, When we got into camp another storm came on, and all ranks were very miserable and wet through. It is a curious sensation to be on the open veldt month after month without any shelter, and we are lucky not to have had more bad weather. Albemarle, who had come on, managed to get us 21 pairs of trousers and 56 shirts in the town. We gave every man five grains of quinine, and, later, a tot of rum. The wet has brought on Edis an attack of fever, and he was so loth to leave his company I had to order him to take shelter in a house.

June 22.—Bitterly cold night and morning. We leave behind here no less than 126 men, who are unfit to go on, fifty-three of them being slight cases of exhaustion and sore feet, and seventy-three being cases of collapse—utter collapse. The poor fellows are completely done, and many had struggled on longer than they should have done. Edis is no better, and I have reluctantly to leave him behind with the bad cases, who will go to Johannesburg, and Garnett, who is not quite fit, goes to Germiston with the slight cases. Sorry though I am to leave so many behind, there is nothing in it discreditable to the battalion, as I am sure there is no malingering; and Sleman tells me that some of the men had tears in their eyes, so loth were they to "go sick."

We marched at 7.30 twelve miles towards Heidelberg. When we got to camp, we saw Boers on the hills to the south, and our "cow" guns opened on them at about 7000 yards. Some of our men were shot at, too, on wood fatigue.

Sergeant Hall, who was wounded at Doorn Kop, rejoined us to-day, and brought news of the death of Privates Wallis and Day from enteric. The latter I had taken special interest in; he was managing partner of Day's Library in Mount Street, London. Our strength in camp to-night is 22 officers and 604 men—total, 626.

I begin thirty-one years' service in the army to-day, and Arnold and the officers drank my health in ration rum.

June 23.—We marched at 7 A.M. to Heidelberg, the Boers having evacuated the hill they were on; we arrived at the railway station at

1 o'clock, and moved into bivouac beyond the engine shed, leaving one company in the shed itself. The mounted infantry had a smart fight, driving Boers off the kopjes east of the town. General Ian Hamilton broke his collar bone while riding about looking at the fight. This is the prettiest town I have seen in South Africa, with a very picturesque Dutch church, and there are many Scots here.

I received the following cablegram from the Lord Mayor—"Most cordial congratulations on Field Marshal's generous praise to battalion. The City very proud of their regiment, but deeply grieved at your losses and wounded. Convey latter sympathy and wire their progress.—Alfred Newton, Lord Mayor." This message gives great pleasure to all ranks, and is dated 17th June. Our march to-day was eight miles.

CHAPTER X

HEIDELBERG TO HEILBRON

June 24.—We could have put up all the battalion in the engine shed last night, but the men preferred sleeping on the veldt. A very cold night again, with a sharp frost: that thunderstorm has quite changed the weather.

We hear that De Wet has burnt three weeks' mails—a most uncivilised act, and one that will be specially hard on our men, who get so much tobacco by parcel post.

We found two big outposts and the town guard—more than half the battalion. Sent two cyclists into Johannesburg with a cable for the Lord Mayor; they are also to inquire after our wounded.

June 25.—Our morning state to-day shows 4 officers and 385 men absent, wounded, and sick, of whom, however, many are convalescent, but unable to get back to us. Our strength in South Africa is 1013 (infantry battalion) as against 1048 on 1st March, the difference being mostly accounted for by nine deaths and twenty-one men invalided home. I wrote to General Hamilton saying that the men are unfit for much hard work, and suggesting that, if tactical considerations permit, they may have at least a week's rest with good food. He came over to see me about it, and told me that, although the work we may be called upon to do may be hard, it will probably not be prolonged, and that, if it is, he will try to get us a rest later: so I am satisfied. I explained that I only wrote because I thought it my duty to tell him how overstrained the men are, and that I acted on the advice of the medical officer.

A letter to-day from the Military Secretary says Moëller, Browne, Burnside, Greene, and Croft are selected for commissions in the army.

June 26.—A telegram from the Military Secretary offers a commission in the West India Regiment to Corporal Wright, who accepts it. This makes thirteen commissions

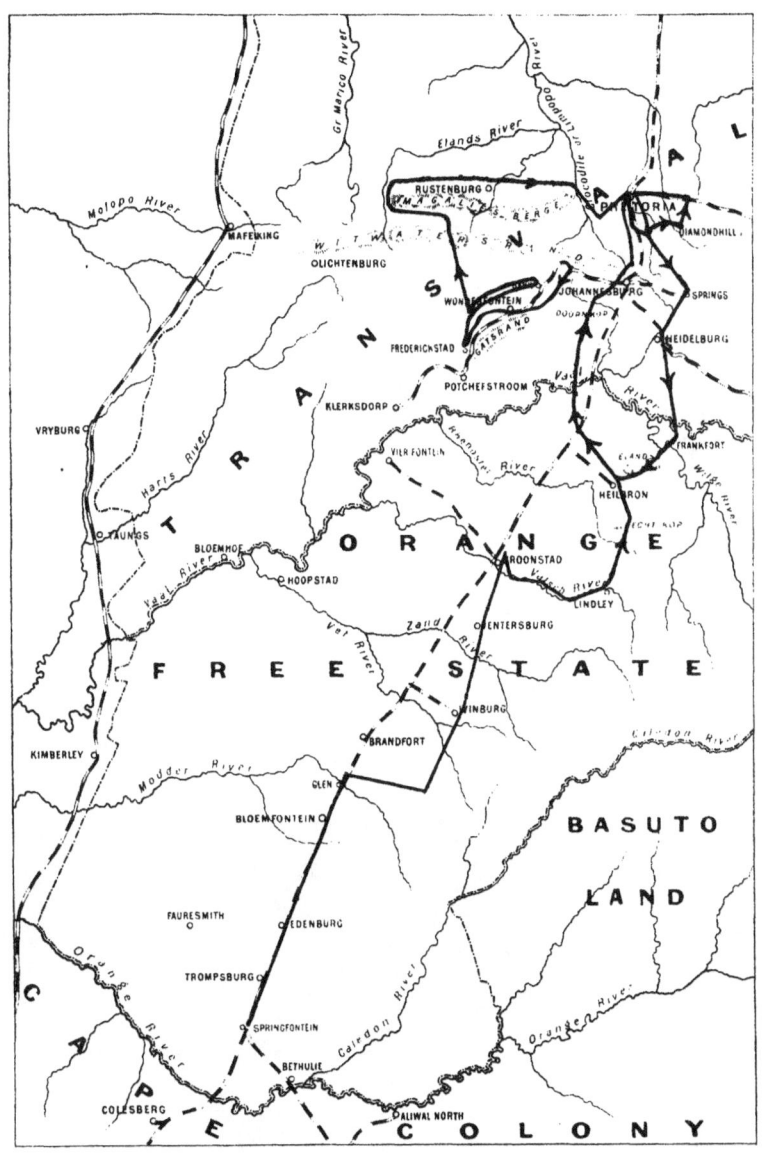

MAP TO ILLUSTRATE THE MARCH OF THE INFANTRY BATTALION OF THE C.I.V.

already given or promised in the City Imperial Volunteers. The cyclists returned late last night, and report that the wounded and sick are doing well. I also hear that Mosley, the barrister private, has made a good beginning, as he not only prosecutes for the Crown, but advises every one on legal points, including the judge on the bench!

I lunched with "Smiler" Kennedy of the Camerons at the Railway Station Bar, and dined with Colonel Waldron, R.A.

June 27.—On the trek again. We were rear-guard of a convoy which consisted of 171 ox-waggons, stretching for five miles, and as the Boers are all round us, it would have been a trying job had we been attacked; but we were not.

My guard consisted of C.I.V., 76th Battery, and 400 mounted infantry, including 200 Scottish Yeomanry, whose newly arrived English horses it is a pleasure to see. The convoy oxen were very exhausted, and many died on the road; so, although we started at noon, we did not arrive at our bivouac till 7 P.M. (twelve miles).

We are due south of Heidelberg, near the Oceana Coal Mine, and just south of the Tukerboschrand River. Sir A. Hunter is now in command of our force *vice* Ian Hamilton.

June 28.—We marched eleven miles south to Bierlaagte, and saw nothing of interest on the way. We got a Johannesburg paper, which notifies that Mr. Mosley, C.I.V., has been made a lieutenant on his appointment as Crown prosecutor.

June 29.—A long and tiresome march of eighteen miles to the Vaal River, through very uninteresting country, flat and treeless. We halt on the river bank facing Villiersdorp. Bitterly cold all day. I walked the whole distance and never once felt warm.

June 30.—The biting easterly wind is still blowing, with sharp frost at night. It took seven hours to get the transport across the river, the battalion crossing by a pontoon. We marched seven miles south.

The cyclists have been doing splendid work lately, taking mails, telegrams, &c., to and from Johannesburg and other places. They

SOME OF THE CYCLIST SECTION

Photo by L. Green Wilkinson

To face p. 118

have frequently taken letters thirty-five miles across the veldt under conditions which were none too safe. They are always eager to go anywhere, and neither risk nor distance is too much for them. It is a pleasure to have such men.

Our rear was engaged with some of the enemy to-day, and the pompoms came into action. Some portion of our force is engaged nearly every day, but I don't, as a rule, allude to it, as the Boers are too slim to stay when we return their fire.

July 1.—I was in command of rear-guard, consisting of C.I.V., 82nd field battery, and 5th mounted infantry. We had to guard the convoy, but no attack was made.

We marched into Frankfort (twelve miles) and camped in the town, on the river Wilge. From seventy to eighty of our convoy animals dropped on the march, and had to be left behind, probably to die.

July 2.—My thermometer showed ten degrees of frost last night, and our bodies on the ground probably experienced greater cold still. We have a rest to-day, which is more welcome than ever, and our ration meat is mutton, which is a boon, as we have had nothing but beef for thirty-five days.

We had a sing-song to-night, which was largely attended, and which was appreciated. Reid acted as M.C., and sang a topical song to the tune of "As we go marching to Georgia," the chorus of which was "Hurrah for the Camerons, so bold and so free; hurrah, hurrah for Sussex and Derby; hurrah for the mounted infantry and the good old C.I.V., as we go marching from Pretoria." Jonah also sang two songs, one of which has for its refrain, "That is the motto for every man" (one of his mottoes was "Never throw a biscuit away").

July 3.—The weather is quite changed, and is now cloudy and windy, and the sun's power has much decreased. This is a nuisance, as De Wet has captured the warm clothing intended for us, and we have no tents. Corporal Wood opened communication by telegraph with Heilbron, and was at work most of the night sending or receiving messages.

Ted went to one of the best houses in the

town, and insisted on a bath being prepared for me. When I went there later, accompanied by my servant Jackson, with soap, towel, and water, the lady of the house received me and showed me to her bedroom, where a tin tub was put out, and in that I scrubbed myself fairly clean. The romance is rather spoilt when I add that the Dutch lady was not above receiving payment for it. General Bruce Hamilton dined with us.

July 4.—Orders were received for us to leave the 21st Brigade (which was going south), and to escort a convoy west to Heilbron. MacKinnon's force, as it is henceforth called, consists of a section of guns of the Royal Artillery (76th battery), 70 scouts of the Eastern Province Horse, 150 of the 5th Mounted Infantry, and the C.I.V. battalion, besides many details.

On leaving the town we were a good deal shot at by the Boers from the hills to the east, but our only casualty was one horse shot dead. Three miles out we captured 300 sheep, and took them along with us. My convoy stretches for four miles, and includes

4000 animals of all sorts. We halted at a spruit, twelve miles out, half of the battalion having to go on outpost. Killed forty-five of our sheep.

July 5.—Fifteen degrees of frost last night and a thick fog this morning. We started at 8 A.M., and very anxious work it was with a long convoy in such darkness. We marched twenty-one miles, and arrived at Heilbron at 5 P.M., being continually shot at, and having at one time to bring our Royal Artillery guns into action on our right flank. I was glad enough to get my charge safely in. Colonel Ewart, Commandant, came out to meet us, and showed us our camp. Another bitter night.

CHAPTER XI

AT HEILBRON

[DE WET, who had been hemmed in against the Drakensberg Mountains, on the south side of the Orange Free Colony, by Hunter, had escaped northwards through the cordon, and passing Heilbron fifteen miles to the south, had crossed the main line of railway in a north-westerly direction, near Rhenoster, closely followed by Broadwood and Little's cavalry brigades.]

July 6.—We got some sixty sacks of mails from the station, an accumulation of three weeks. To my horror, I received a telegram from the Chief of the Staff, saying the C.I.V. were to go on escort again to-morrow. I had hoped for at least four or five days' rest; so I wired to Lord Kitchener: "C.I.V. urgently in need of rest. Suggest Argyll and Sutherland Highlanders find escort." And he replied: "Your suggestion approved."

I am governor and commander-in-chief of this town, and my army consists, in addition to what I brought in, of the Argyll and Sutherland Highlanders, five companies of a provisional battalion, and two large 4.7 naval guns under Commander Grant, R.N. Ted has ordered one of the largest houses in the town to prepare for my reception. It belongs to Mr. Pearce, an Englishman, and I take there with me Ted, Orr, our servants, and probably all our horses.

Kitchener's telegram so alarms me (after General Bruce Hamilton having told me that we should certainly have a rest here) that I have sent Arnold to Pretoria with a letter, pointing out that the men are in rags, that they are footsore and quite broken-down, and that the present strength of the battalion is 570, as against 1045 who landed in South Africa in February last.

I received 350 letters to-day, nearly all of an official nature, and the weight of my mail was fifty pounds.

We handed over three prisoners whom we caught yesterday to the provost-marshal. One of my mounted infantry took one of them cleverly and red-handed, for he was shooting at us when this man rode round, crept behind, and got within five yards. The Boer then threw down his rifle, which proved to be an English Lee-Metford.

July 7.—I hardly know myself this morning, waking up in a large bedroom, and being in pyjamas and between sheets, which has not been my lot for nearly six months. I had breakfast in bed at 7 o'clock. The Argyll and Sutherland Highlanders proceeded on escort duty, so we moved into their quarters near the station, having six companies on detachment round the town. I went to visit them and the Naval Brigade in the afternoon.

Colonel Ewart dined with us, and during the evening a despatch rider arrived from Lord Methuen asking for news (he is forty miles south), and a Mr. Wilson came in. He is a resident of Heilbron, and has been a prisoner with the Boers for a month. He gave a great deal of information about the movements of the enemy.

July 8.—I don't sleep at all well in my official

residence, as a room (even in ten degrees of frost) feels so warm, and I have a dry mouth when I wake up. It is delightful to see what a change the rest, and getting their mails, has made in officers and men. It is already quite an altered battalion, though there are many limpers still about. We had breakfast at 8 A.M., and voluntary divine service was held by each company.

The result of an interview with Mr. Wilson is that we learn that the main body of the Boers has retired from Bethlehem due south to Fouriesburg (thirty-five miles), close to the mountains on the Basutoland border; that they are simply holding out till the result of the American elections is known (this is incredible, but Mr. Wilson assures us it is absolutely true, and that many friends in America tell them they will soon be relieved by an American army); that they are issuing paper currency, and that Lord Roberts' proclamation is being studiously withheld from the people. He also says that several Free State officials, including the State-Attorney, are coming in to surrender to me to-day.

AT HEILBRON

July 9.—I had an interesting interview yesterday with the officials whom I expected, and who came in and surrendered, among them being State-Secretary Blignaut, State-Attorney Dickson, and three members of the Volksraad, including Mr. Luyt, member for Heilbron. I put them on parole, and wired in cypher to Lord Roberts, asking if they could be allowed to go to their homes near Bloemfontein. They gave me much information of interest, and it seems impossible that the war about here can last much longer. Twenty-nine men, in addition, came in from a laager to-day, and handed in their rifles.

I rode round the outposts of the town, and discovered a clansman from Skye in the Cameron Highlanders, with whom I made great friends, and a fine-looking man he was. Our numbers to-day are only 569, of whom 30 are unfit; this does not include officers.

July 10.—Arnold returned from Pretoria, but, alas! his mission was fruitless, and we are to march again as soon as the convoy comes in. Lord Kitchener says it was a mistake ordering us to find the escort directly we arrived, but he won't hear of our staying here to rest and reclothe the men, so we must go in rags, unless Matthey manages to rejoin us, which I doubt.

A cypher message arrived from Lord Roberts to say that Mr. Blignaut only, of the political prisoners, may go to Bloemfontein; the remainder are to be exiled to Durban. I arranged a meeting with them, and told them their fate, which does not please them. A few more Boers came in and gave up their arms.

I visited the hospital, and saw some bad cases, one of the worst being Lieutenant Innes, Black Watch, who was wounded at Magersfontein, went home, and got well, then on the voyage out again contracted pneumonia, was nearly convalescent, and then got enteric, which now has a bad hold of him.

Triggs returned to Bloemfontein to-day, taking 29 men with him who will be unfit to march. Lee, my orderly, is one of them, with water on the knee. This is the third orderly I have had, and he is the second of them who has had to go sick, much to my regret.

July 11.—The Argyll and Sutherland High-

OUR AMBULANCE

Photo by Capt. Orr

To face p. 128

AT HEILBRON

landers returned from Wolverhoek to-day, after escorting the convoy.

The empty convoy, which we are to escort back, arrived to-day under Colonel Cunningham, with an escort of 1000 men, including the Derby Regiment. A telegram to-night from the Chief of the Staff, that the C.I.V. are to remain to garrison Heilbron, and the Argyll and Sutherland Highlanders to proceed forthwith to Pretoria. I am very glad of this for the sake of the men, who still require rest and new clothing. Am sending two more typewriters to Lord Roberts.

July 12.—Up to date, 1 officer and 33 men of the C.I.V. have died in South Africa, and 3 officers and 74 men have been invalided home. They are distributed as follows:—

Killed or Died.

	Officers Killed.	Men Killed.	Enteric.	Otherwise.
Battery	—	—	—	—
Mounted Infantry	—	2	10	3
Infantry	1	2	15	1

Invalided home.

	Officers.	Men.
Battery	—	2
Mounted Infantry	1	32
Infantry	2	40

I

I am glad to say that I have, up to now, secured no less than eighteen commissions for this regiment, which, I think, is very creditable to the corps. As I hope there are yet more to come, I will postpone recording the names.[1] Orr takes over the duties of railway staff officer. Busy all day loading up the convoy waggons for General Hunter.

Colonel Cunningham proceeded to-day to Pretoria, also the Argyll and Sutherland Highlanders in two special trains of open trucks. The strength of my command last night was nearly 3000. Garnett came over from Germiston, but was not given leave to stay, as no details are allowed to rejoin their units.

July 13.—The convoy left here to-day to rejoin General Hunter. Colonel Ewart commanded it, and all the troops in garrison went with him except the C.I.V.'s., the two Naval 4.7 guns, the Provisional Battalion, and 100 of the Eastern Province Horse.

July 14.—To our great joy Matthey arrived this morning from Bloemfontein with a truckload of some 800 complete suits and shirts,

[1] See Appendix.

AT HEILBRON

&c., and we began unloading and fitting at once, completing five companies before dark.

Private Haggard, cyclist, of the Inns of Court, received a commission as Lieutenant in the C.I.V., and began his new duties to-day.

July 15.—Church parade, which the Naval Brigade, under Commander Grant, also attended. Mr. Day, who has been appointed chaplain to the troops, officiated; he is a minister in the town.

The 3rd Cavalry Brigade marched in from Reitz. My orders had been to put them in the train for Pretoria, and Orr had eight special trains up the line awaiting them; but, just before they arrived, these instructions were cancelled, and the brigade was ordered instead to march south to Winburg. General Gordon was directed to go to Springs to take over the 1st Cavalry Brigade, and left by special train at 7.30 P.M. The cavalry remain here to-night, excepting 170 sick horses, and some dismounted men, who go to Kroonstad.

Marsh left for Pretoria for civil employment. We are all sorry to lose him, though I hope it will be to his advantage. Corporal Beirne also went with him. A cable from our Depôt says, "18 battery, 19 mounted, 110 infantry, 3 infantry officers sailed yesterday *Ulstermore*." With the cavalry to-day came eighty Boer prisoners, and 200 sick and wounded of ours from Bethlehem.

July 16.—The 3rd Cavalry Brigade marched off at 9 A.M., leaving their camping-ground strewn with dead horses and oxen. Boers continue to give in their arms, some 200 having done so in the last week. They are all given passes to go out of the town, and there is no guarantee that they don't have new arms issued to them, and that some of them don't come in simply to gain information.

Ten convalescents joined us to-day from various places. We played the Eastern Province Horse at cricket, but were sadly beaten. Among our team were Jonah, Reid, John Orr, and Treffry.

July 17.—An order from the Chief of the Staff to send a messenger at once to catch up 3rd Cavalry Brigade, and to divert them to Lindley, as Boers have broken through cordon

AT HEILBRON

at Stabbert's Nek. Sent four Eastern Province Horse.

The strength of our garrison to-day is a little over 1600, including 330 sick and wounded. The Provisional Battalion numbers 450, the Naval Brigade 50, Eastern Province Horse 90, Yeomanry 36, and Royal Engineers 67.

July 18.—Sorry to hear of Corporal Jones's (H. Company) death from enteric yesterday in the hospital here; he was buried this morning.

Part of our English mail arrived. An important message came in from Lord Roberts, telling me to at once send messengers to catch General Broadwood or Colonel Little, to say they must co-operate in attacking De Wet, who has escaped through our cordon, and is now trekking north-east somewhere near Lindley. I sent off two men of Eastern Province Horse, and also, at a different time, two cyclists, Gascoigne and Henderson. It is a risky ride for them, over at least fifty miles of veldt.

The four Eastern Province Horse whom I sent after Little yesterday morning returned at 9.30 A.M. They caught him up forty miles on the road to Kroonstad; therefore they covered eighty miles during the twenty-four hours, and came in comparatively fresh, with a new horse, which they commandeered to take the place of one which broke down.

Mortimore went to Pretoria, &c., to see our sick and wounded. Lord Kitchener called me up on the wire from Kroonstad to ask me various questions as to the strength of our garrison.

July 19.—A telegram arrived this morning from the Director of Military Intelligence to say De Wet is reported to be making for Heilbron. I met the commanding officers this afternoon, and we took special measures for defence, moving one of the two naval guns to the Kaffir Kraal, 2000 yards south of the naval camp, and strengthening our outposts generally, and the town guards as much as possible.

There was a marked diminution in the number of civilians who came into town to-day, and at 5.30 P.M. our wire to Kroonstad was cut—both suspicious circumstances. We all slept at our posts. I had telegrams from Lord Roberts and reports from our outposts through the night, and at 5 A.M. we stood to arms. It was a bitterly cold and very foggy morning. There were no signs of the enemy.

July 20.—Our patrols fail to give us any news this morning. A wire received from Lord Roberts to send four messengers in different directions to find Little and Broadwood, urging them to catch up De Wet, who is supposed to be taking Steyn with him northeast to the Pretoria-Delagoa line.

Our strength to-day is 23 officers and 562 men. We are slowly increasing in numbers, as a few men come back to us now and again.

About 8 P.M. a native came into the town and reported that there were many Boers on Spitzkop, seven miles south, and that they were going to attack us to-night or early to-morrow. We all slept at our posts again to-night.

July 21.—No alarms. At 6 A.M. the two Eastern Province Horse despatch riders, whom I sent to Little on the 18th returned, having found him at 10 A.M. on 19th. They brought a letter from him saying he had a fight on the 19th and drove off the Boers, who apparently retired north towards the Rhenoster River, and that he is following them. Broadwood's whereabouts are not known.

Several runners come in and report Boers all round us, 700 being seen on Eland's Kop (north), 200 on the Frankfort Road (east), and a quantity on Spitzkop (south), besides De Wet's commando on the west. About 6 P.M. rockets were mysteriously sent up from some parts of the town. There were many rumours too among the Kaffirs of an impending night attack by De Wet, so that it was a time of considerable anxiety. I ordered all civilians' lights in the town to be put out by 8 P.M., and Ted made midnight domiciliary visits with the garrison military police to various suspected houses.

July 22.—Again no alarm during the night, for which we were all thankful. The two despatch riders whom I sent on 20th to try to find Broadwood returned; they went twenty-five miles out and back, but could not get through, and only just escaped capture after being pursued for eight miles.

Glad to hear by letter from the Military Secretary that Castle Smith, my orderly, Haggard, and Cadell are all to have commissions in the regular army.

A telegram from Lord Roberts says that De Wet has blown up the line between Honingspruit and Roodewal, and that I am to send two more messengers to Broadwood, who is believed to be at Vaalkranz, to tell him to proceed at once to Roodewal. Sent two Eastern Province Horse, but getting a message soon after they had started, from Broadwood from Rhenoster, I was able to recall them.

July 23.—Such a bombshell this morning! I received a wire from the Chief of the Staff ordering me at once to remove all the garrison and supplies to Krugersdorp. Orr estimates this will mean at least eight long trains, and as this is a single line, it will take probably twenty-four hours' continuous work. And as the Boers are all around, it will not be easy to withdraw and entrain the last lot of men.

Was busy all day. Wired to Kitchener to ask leave to poison the 4000 sheep and 400 slaughter oxen we have got, in order to prevent their falling into the hands of the enemy. Had to arrange for a local medico to take charge of twenty-eight dying patients belonging to many different regiments, whom we cannot move. Took £6000 in notes and gold from the bank to prevent the Boers getting it. I told a deputation of loyalists, who are miserable at the withdrawal of the garrison, that I would take any of them away with me who cared to come. We burnt some hundreds of Mauser rifles which had been taken from the Boers.

These were a few of the things which took up time, and besides these, the loading and despatching of trains went on all night. The first train left at 7.30 P.M., all supplies, with Green's Company as escort, and fifty sick.

July 24.—A certain amount of firing last night. One civilian was wounded twice in the leg for giving the wrong countersign, and our patrols and pickets were sniped. The second

AT HEILBRON

train left at 3 A.M.; the third, with Albemarle, at 7.45.

So far our efforts at the quick despatch of trains has not been successful, and it is assuredly not due to lack of hard work. Orr was at it all night, and had frequently to stir up the slow station-master; I, too, never shut my eyes. But a branch single line of twenty-eight miles, with no siding during all its length, is difficult to work; also, oxen are not easy animals to load, and we could only fill one truck at a time. At 1 P.M. the assistant-director of railways (Major Murray, R.E.) arrived. At first he was surprised at our slow progress, but he soon saw that we were doing all we could.

Noticing, during the middle of the day, parties of Boers moving along the hills towards the railway line, and hearing renewed rumours that they meant to wreck one of our trains, I arrested four of the principal residents and confined them in a waiting-room at the station, at the same time causing it to be widely known in the town that, should a British soldier lose his life by any wrecking of trains, the hostages I had (one was to be placed with a guard in the front of each night train) would be shot dead.

They were terribly frightened at this, and three out of the four turned deadly pale, one of them, Mr. Elsa, at once asking for a pass for a friend of his (De Kock, one of the most ill-favoured looking ruffians I ever saw) to go out through the outposts to the hills to stop any attack. I gave it to him, and he went out as hard as he could, taking a bee line in a particular direction, and evidently knowing all about the Boer patrols' whereabouts.

The next train went at 4 P.M.; then we began on the Naval Brigade, with their huge guns, and got them off at 11 P.M. with a strong escort of C.I.V.'s under Bailey. In this train also went the refugees, some forty in number, who were afraid to stay behind; the prisoners of war (forty-five) and those (political and otherwise) who are on parole; also a Mrs. Menger, a Dutch lady, who had threatened that, as soon as the Boers came into the town, she would have some of the British sympathisers killed. When my escort for her arrived she was mad with rage, at first refused to leave her house,

EVACUATING HEILBRON

Photo by L. Green Wilkinson

To face p. 140

and then became very violent, saying she would like to see every d——d English soldier shot. I arranged with the Commissioner to have her sent to Kroonstad, where she will be harmless.

CHAPTER XII

HEILBRON TO FREDERICKSTADT

[DE WET was still on his way north with Steyn near Vredefort, with Knox, Broadwood, and Little closely in touch. The rest of the army which he had left behind on the Basuto border had surrendered to Hunter. Buller's force had crossed from Natal, and was moving north-west along the Natal Railway.]

July 25.—The sixth train completed the Naval Brigade and the C.I.V. with some of the Eastern Province Horse; and I came away in this myself. We got off at 2.30 A.M., officers and men being all huddled up together in empty coal trucks. The hostage in this train was the head Dutch minister, who is very anti-British. We arrived at Johannesburg at 4 P.M., where I was glad to hand over the money to a bank clerk who met me, and at Krugersdorp at 6 P.M. A violent thunderstorm broke over us just as we arrived in our open trucks, and wet us through, and the night was piercingly cold, with rain and wind.

Albemarle met us, and showed the way, and had kindly got a "tap-room" in some empty drinking saloon for me to lie down in, and glad I was to get into it. Quentin Agnew also met me. He is Provost-Marshal here.

July 26.—Delighted to find the two last trains from Heilbron had got away safely. They arrived here during the night. But the last one found something wrong on the line near Heilbron, and the train having been stopped, it was discovered that some of the fishplates had been removed; so there was some devilry about, and I think the taking of those four leading inhabitants has quite likely prevented a "wreck."

It is a great relief to have got the 2000 souls and those piles of supplies away without a hitch, and I cannot speak too highly of Orr's great energy. It was forty-five hours from the time of arrival of our first train at Heilbron to the time of departure of the last, and during all that time he worked incessantly day and night, and it was entirely due to him that we got away as quickly as we did. Dined with the General (Barton) and Agnew.

July 27.—This is a bleak, cold, ugly country, with chimneys and heaps of quartz and slack in every direction. But the mines are idle, and only in a few of them is even pumping going on.

I am going to Johannesburg this afternoon to see the Military Governor about my Heilbron prisoners. I had hardly written these words when an order came for us to proceed by train to join Lord Methuen about twenty-five miles west. We loaded up our baggage and the mules of our first line transport in the afternoon.

July 28.—We leave Burnside behind, who goes to England at once, before joining the 3rd Hussars. We are sorry to lose him; he has been a great deal with head-quarters from the time of leaving England. Matthey also stays behind with a bad foot, and about eighteen sick men.

We paraded at 5.45 A.M., taking our first

HEILBRON TO FREDERICKSTADT

line transport with us, the second line going empty by road with G. and H. Companies as escort. We arrived at Bank at 9.30 and marched to our bivouac. We are under Smith-Dorrien, whose only other battalion at present is the Shropshire. Methuen went on yesterday towards Potchefstroom.

Lord Kitchener was at the station when we entrained this morning, and I had a long talk with him. He appreciated all the C.I.V. had done, and said we had well earned our rest; he does not seem pleased, on reflection, at his action in withdrawing the garrison from Heilbron, for he says Wolverhoek is already nearly surrounded by Heilbron commandoes.

No news, I am sorry to say, of our cyclist despatch riders, Gascoigne and Henderson, who left us on 18th, and I am reporting them as missing.

July 29.—G. and H. Companies marched in early with the convoy. At 2 P.M. the whole force moved off alongside the rail westward, and halted at Wonderfontein, eight miles.

July 30.—We marched eighteen miles to Frederickstadt. On arrival there with the advance guard, I heard a continuous whistle of a railway train, and being sure that something was wrong I galloped across, and found our supply train had been wrecked by the Boers. It was a terrible sight. We picked out nine bodies while I was there, and seven more were subsequently found under the trucks. Nearly all of these were men of the Shropshires, 100 of whom were on the train rejoining the battalion, and some were volunteers fresh from England. Forty were injured, some of them very badly. This may be war, but it was very shocking to see those poor fellows laid out in a row, frightfully knocked about, as a rule, in the head.

WRECKED TRAIN, FREDERICKSTADT. STEAM STILL ISSUING FROM FUNNEL

Photo by Capt. Orr

CHAPTER XIII

AT FREDERICKSTADT

[DE WET was still on his way to the Vaal, and close to it.]

July 31.—I was still in my blankets at 7 A.M. when Jonah brought up two Boers, armed and mounted, with a white flag, who quietly said, "I am sent by my commandant, Lieberberg, to ask for the surrender of your force within half-an-hour. On resigning your arms and ammunition, you will be allowed to go to Potchefstroom!" Rubbing my eyes, I looked at the man who spoke, and hardly thought he was in earnest; I felt sure he must be drunk. I sent him on to head-quarters, but before he got there firing began between the Boers and our outposts to the south-west of the camp. Jonah and I rode on alone to our outpost to ascertain the direction from which the enemy were coming, and suddenly found ourselves 400 yards from twelve mounted Boers, who fired at us. Galloping back, I hurriedly got up five companies and two guns (which were for the time under my orders), and the enemy, who had for the moment gained a footing on the hills above our camp, were soon driven back.

They retired in a westerly direction, and I followed them for a couple of miles, one well-directed shell from one of my guns emptying four saddles at 4500 yards. We then heard Methuen's guns coming from Potchefstroom, which had evidently got in touch with the Boers after hearing from us by heliograph ; so we gave up our pursuit, and went on to meet what turned out to be a convoy of empty waggons sent by Methuen for supplies which had been brought by the wrecked train.

I am sorry to say we had two men killed to-day, W. H. Shrimpton and C. J. Day, both of B. Company, and the following severely wounded: W. A. Thick and H. Hunt of A. Company, and J. A. Robinson and L. Streat

AT FREDERICKSTADT

of E. Company. They were hit in the spine, head, thigh, and forehead respectively. It is unfortunate that the only men hit should have been killed or severely wounded.

We were back in camp by 2 P.M. Afterwards Ted and I went over to see our wounded in hospital, then attended the funeral of all the Shropshire men who were killed in the railway wreck; then went to see the General, who showed me a despatch he was sending to Lord Roberts, in which he spoke most highly of the C.I.V.'s behaviour to-day, and at 5 o'clock we rode on to the kopje where our two poor fellows were killed.

It is well situated about two miles northeast of the village of Frederickstadt, with a good view of what is quite pretty country all round, and here, with the sun setting in a very red sky, I read the burial service, and we laid the bodies in the ground, inside a stone sangar on the summit of the hill, at the exact spot where they were killed. It is sad to think that both these men died while trying to minister to a wounded yeoman. Day was a stretcher-bearer (without even a rifle in his hand), and on Green telling him a yeoman was wounded close by, he jumped up to go to his assistance, and was at once killed with a bullet through his head. Green then asking for a volunteer to take his place, Shrimpton got up, and was also at once hit in the middle of the body, and only lived half-an-hour. In all our actions the stretcher-bearers have behaved splendidly.

August 1.—I went over to see the wounded to-day, and found them all doing well. Streat's is a wonderful case, the bullet having gone in at the right temple, then passed clean through the right eye, and out at the forehead; yet the man is marvellously cheerful, and all he complains of is being unable to eat the hard biscuit, which, alas! is all he can get here, for we are isolated from the world—rail and telegraph being hopelessly cut. I issued the following regimental order to-day :—

" The Commandant much regrets the deaths in action yesterday of Private W. H. Shrimpton and Private C. J. Day, both of B. Company. These men met with their deaths while endeavouring to minister to a wounded yeoman who

OUR STRETCHER-BEARERS

Photo by L. Green Wilkinson

To face p. 150

was lying close by, and the Commandant is much gratified at being able again to remark on the self-sacrifice and devotion shown by Surgeon-Captain Sleman and the regimental stretcher-bearers, who miss the excitement of being in the firing line, and yet are far more exposed than if they were there. Major-General Smith-Dorrien has expressed his great satisfaction with the rapidity with which the battalion turned out yesterday, and with the way in which it behaved, and he has so informed the Field Marshal Commanding-in-Chief."

We sent one company to guard the Royal Engineers who were repairing a broken railway bridge near Frederickstadt, and Albemarle took three companies, twenty-five Yeomanry, and two guns to see the convoy safely on its way to Potchefstroom.

August 2.—The weather is getting distinctly warmer by day, and the nights are much less cold, though there was a sharp frost last night. All the men clear of duty were occupied to-day in improving our defences. Pawle took two companies and some Yeomanry to meet a reinforcement coming to us from Lord Methuen. I saw our wounded; they are doing marvellously well, and will, I trust, all recover.

We are still isolated from the world, and, with the numbers of Boers there are all around us, are likely to remain so.

August 3.—Half the Shropshires with two guns and some Yeomanry left us to-day for Welverdiend.

August 4.—Three commandoes of Boers are round the village of Boshop, three miles off. We were on the alert in case of attack. I took out two guns and some Yeomanry, and we opened fire on them; they retired out of range, but remained watching us, ultimately withdrawing towards their laager, some six miles north-west of our camp, which we can see plainly. There were many fires and lights all round us to-night. Arnold and I dined with the General.

I found Poynter of the Yeomanry lying wounded in a platelayer's cottage: the bullet went in at his side, and remains imbedded in the lung, but he is doing wonderfully well, and

AT FREDERICKSTADT 153

the doctor hopes that tissue is growing round it, and that he will soon be convalescent.

August 5.—This is Sunday, but with the anxious night-work our men have, church parade is out of the question. Our wounded are all doing well. The Yeomanry patrol were fired on, and two men dangerously wounded.

Fitzclarence started by night on his cycle for Bank, with a letter from the General Officer Commanding.

We have been now for two days on short rations, and this seems likely to continue. One compensation, however, is that we are getting mutton, or rather goat-mutton, which we kill ourselves—seventy or eighty animals a day, each of which averages under 20 lbs. weight. The quartermaster has weighed for me what each of our men has been carrying on his person during the campaign. The total reaches to $41\frac{1}{4}$ lbs., of which the rifle accounts for $9\frac{1}{2}$ lbs., the waistbelt, bayonet, shirt, socks, mess-kettle and meat ration $11\frac{1}{2}$ lbs., the bandolier and haversack $13\frac{3}{4}$ lbs., and the water-bottle and one of the entrenching tools $6\frac{1}{2}$ lbs.

August 6.—The General intends to move to Potchefstroom to-morrow, leaving me in command here, so I have been busy all day taking over the work.

August 7.—The General was to have started this morning, but the train coming in from Welverdiend was attacked half way out and driven back. Directly we heard this, nearly all our force started off, drove the enemy back, and got the train in by 6 P.M. One Yeoman was dangerously wounded, and Sergeant Marsh was crushed rather badly by a trolley going over him.

A great many camp fires and veldt fires round us to-night.

August 8.—Hearing from Methuen that De Wet had crossed the Vaal and was moving north, Smith-Dorrien, in accordance with orders from Pretoria, returns to Bank with all his force. So instructions were secretly issued at 6 P.M. to march at 9, and leave all our camp fires burning, and not to show any lights, or to make any noise during the march. We did not get well under weigh till 10 P.M., half of H. Company having gone three miles

AT FREDERICKSTADT

up the line to guard a railway culvert, and having to get back. B. and G. Companies, which had been for two days holding a kopje three miles east, also returned and marched with us.

CHAPTER XIV

BETWEEN FREDERICKSTADT AND BANK

[DE WET has crossed the Vaal, and is moving north through the Gatsrand.]

August 9.—We kept on in the moonlight till 2.30 A.M., when we lay down near Welverdiend Station till 9; we then resumed our march, and arrived at Bank at 3 P.M.—a good performance of thirty miles in seventeen hours. The men were very exhausted, and about twenty fell out on the way. Edis and fifty-five men, nearly all convalescents, joined us from Germiston in the evening. The following telegram was received late at night from Lord Roberts:—

"Congratulate Shropshires for me on march, forty-three miles in thirty-two hours, and rest of force on doing thirty miles in seventeen hours."

August 10.—An exciting day, for we could hear continual firing on the top of the Gatsrand between De Wet and Methuen, and we could see Boer scouts looking over towards us. Our Yeomanry patrol were in touch with him, and had two men wounded, one of them being also taken prisoner.

The General had Spens (commanding the Shropshires) and me into consultation, and decided to train the Shropshires to Welverdiend after dark, and that the C.I.V. should march, also after dark, half way there. We hoped in this way to intercept De Wet, who is escaping from the Vaal River northward.

Arnold and Ted rode out in the afternoon to settle on our bivouac ground, and were fired at, but luckily not hit. We paraded at 6, and marched seven miles along the railway line to the second ganger's hut, where we stayed the night. We left one officer and forty men at the first hut with a signalling section. I kept up communication by lamp-flashing all night with Smith-Dorrien.

August 11.—I received a message at 5

A.M. to march the battalion to Doornfontein, south of Welverdiend, in order to join Spens.

A Yeomanry patrol which I sent out before daybreak was fired on, and, as soon as it was light, I sent ten shrapnel shells at detached parties of Boers to the north, which stopped their sniping. We had breakfast at 6, and marched soon after, dropping two detachments of one officer and forty men each, at two signalling stations.

On arriving at Doornfontein, Spens told me that De Wet had passed through before he got there, and had crossed the railway, blowing up a culvert and otherwise damaging the line; we decided, therefore, to return to Welverdiend. All ranks were very tired, as we had marched fifteen miles, and have had bad nights lately. I saw and had a talk with Lord Kitchener in the railway station.

We had all got inside our blankets and were fast sleep by 8 P.M., when Colonel Inglefield (Brigade Major) woke me up, and told me we were to send a detachment of four

FREDERICKSTADT AND BANK 159

companies to Bank at once by train. So we had to get everybody up, and Albemarle and 300 men proceeded at 9.30 P.M. The following officers went with him: Captain Mortimore, and Lieutenants Smith, Croft, Jeffery, and Greenwell.

CHAPTER XV

WITH KITCHENER AFTER DE WET

[DE WET, having come through the Gats-rand, and having crossed the railway between Welverdiend and Frederickstadt, continued his flight in a north-westerly direction.]

August 12.—We were told early that we should stay here as garrison, but, as I afterwards learnt, Smith-Dorrien begged Kitchener to let him keep at any rate some C.I.V.'s; so the order was cancelled, and we marched at 9 A.M., our half battalion forming advance guard.

Pawle left us for Pretoria to take up civil employment. As he may possibly rejoin us, all I shall say here is that I am *very* sorry to lose him.

We marched west by north eight miles to Rietvlei, on the north bank of the Mooi River.

WITH KITCHENER AFTER DE WET

We were frequently halted owing to rather confused orders given to the various brigades (Broadwood's, Little's, and ours), and did not get to our bivouac till 5 P.M.

August 13.—The drift over the river was very difficult, and our baggage did not get in till 1 A.M., and as we had breakfast at 2.30, and parade was at 3, there was not much sleep. We marched at 3.10 due north, had an hour and a half's halt at 9, and reached Zwartkop at 3.40 (twenty-five solid miles). This is the longest march we have had, and the men stuck gallantly to it, only thirty falling out. A strong head-wind was blowing all day, and there was a cloud of dust in our faces, and the last four miles were very trying owing to the veldt being so rough. The Shropshires had seventy men fall out, which was the same proportion as ours.

At our early breakfast to-day we had potted grouse, which had been specially sent out to Jonah.

Methuen is some miles ahead of us, and we have frequently heard heavy firing, even after sunset. The moon was at its full this morning—always a lovely sight in this country. I could easily read my pencil-written orders by its light.

August 14.—Our thirty men who fell out yesterday formed part of a sick convoy which returned to-day to Frederickstadt, which is to be our new base.

Our cyclists are doing very hard work, being employed day and night by Lord Kitchener between us and the railway line. Clegg, for instance, left us at 8 P.M. on the 12th for General Hart, then he had to go to Welverdiend, then back to Hart, whom he had to guide by moonlight to the drift, finally coming on himself with Lord Kitchener's despatches. He thus travelled continuously for two days and a night, and, except that General Hart gave him breakfast, he had very little food. He rejoined us at 8 A.M. yesterday on a horse, which had been issued to him at Welverdiend, as his bike had broken down. By our General's leave we retain the horse.

I am delighted to get a telegram saying that Gascoigne and Henderson — the two missing cyclists—are safe, having been taken prisoners, and then escaping.

An order was issued last night as follows:—

"Lord Kitchener asks to express his appreciation of the splendid march made by the troops to-day, who covered twenty-five miles in 12½ hours."

We paraded at 6.15 and marched sixteen miles to Syperwater, where we bivouacked at 3.30. Twenty-seven men fell out, which is hardly to be wondered at, as forty-one miles in two days is good work; and, what is a better record still, we have marched 100 miles in five days 21½ hours.

August 15.—We marched sixteen miles to Leeuwfontein, where we heard, to our great regret, that De Wet had escaped through Oliphant's Nek into the Magaliesburg Mountains; so all our terrific work has been for nothing! It is a great disappointment, and our failure to catch him will surely prolong the war. It is no discredit to the British, for his convoy was mostly composed of Cape carts, whereas ours are ox or mule waggons; then he knows every inch of the country, he can fight a rear-guard action on these kopjes continually, and being in front of us, he can keep on commandeering fresh animals of all kinds.

Late at night a runner arrived from Colonel Hore at Brakfontein, sixteen miles off, to say that he and his 300 Bushmen and Colonials were surrounded by Boers, and unless he was at once relieved he would have to surrender; so sudden orders were issued and—

August 16.—We paraded at 3.45 A.M., and marched to Tweefontein, where, hearing that Colonel Hore was already relieved, we halted for two hours, arriving at Brakfontein at 2 P.M. Only twelve men fell out, which was wonderful. To-day we complete 913 miles, of which the last 132 have been marched in seven days and twenty hours.

The weather now is much hotter, and the country hereabouts is quite pretty, and very fertile, especially in the valleys under the Magaliesburg range. In fact, after over 900 miles of trek, it is the only part of South Africa which I have found attractive.

The following is an extract from Brigade orders :—

"No words can describe the General Officer Commanding's pride at the splendid way in which the infantry have marched. It has drawn forth the admiration of all the mounted branches."

These complimentary orders, though gratifying, do not cure exhaustion or footsoreness, and one of the men was heard to say to-day, "On the trek again. Half rations and full congratulations." We are on three-quarter rations, as a matter of fact, but the beef is so poor and the meal so unbakeable (by amateurs) that the men call it half rations; the forage for animals is also reduced from to-day to half.

August 17.—The most welcome day of rest we have had in South Africa. Pom luckily found two fat pigs yesterday, which will be a valuable supplement to the men's scanty rations. About forty sick to see the doctor this morning, but most of them will be fit by to-morrow.

We have a prisoner in camp—an officer— captured yesterday, who is the head of the Orange Free State detectives, and who was on his way with a letter to De Wet. We have him closely watched, as he gives the impression of wishing to escape. He is a typical Boer, and is surly and unattractive.

General Smith-Dorrien thanked me warmly for the excellent work our cyclists have done, and says they have been invaluable.

It is wonderful how Colonel Hore held out against the large force of Boers. With the smallest amount of pluck they could have rushed his position. As it was, they only kept up a heavy fire, and although they advanced to within 150 yards during the night, they never attempted to get in. His force, which is mostly composed of Rhodesian Horse and Australian Bushmen, was 500 strong, and they held out for a fortnight. Their casualties were sixty, and nearly four hundred horses killed. I went over the position to-day, and it is a very striking one, showing what can be done by marvellous pluck and endurance. The Boers heard of our approach two days ago, and decamped during the night. There were 2000 of them with three guns besieging 500 Colonials with one old 9-pounder gun.

August 18.—This was a tedious day. We

WITH KITCHENER AFTER DE WET 167

were rear-guard to the brigade, which left camp at 4.30 A.M., accompanied by Ridley's Mounted Infantry. There were some difficult spruits to cross, and we did not get to our bivouac at Twei River (eighteen miles) before 8.30 P.M. We passed Methuen's Division about 2 P.M., and I was delighted to see him, Stretty, and Loch, and I lunched at their headquarters. After their hard work it has been desperate bad luck for them not to catch De Wet.

August 19.—We were advance guard to-day, and left camp punctually at 4 A.M., lighted by a waning moon, and helped in our direction by a brilliant Southern Cross. We marched east to the Magaliesburg Hills, where we expected opposition at the Magala Pass, but we got through safely, and arrived at Rustenburg (twenty miles) at 2 P.M. We bivouacked in the Market Square, all the rest of the troops staying outside on the veldt. It is a pretty town, and distinctly semi-tropical in climate and vegetation, palms and oranges flourishing, and the heat being many degrees greater than anything we have yet experienced.

The summit and the slopes of the Magaliesburg are quite beautiful, both in the outlines of the hills and in the flowers, which will soon be at their best. The commonest tree is the Protea, which sheds a bulbous yellow production like an artichoke. It is said that this town was laid out by Kruger, who owns a great deal of land about. Pom and I dined with the General.

August 20.—We marched at 5 A.M., and bivouacked at Hoedspruit (twelve miles).

August 21.—The force marched at 3.30 A.M. We were rear-guard. The moon was too small to give any useful light, and the Southern Cross always seems at these very early starts to be standing on its head, so our direction is not too easy to make out. We halted continuously, and had many difficult drifts.

Our principal duties were to put out of their misery the many dying animals left behind by the column, and to awaken all the exhausted men who had dropped asleep on the veldt. It was altogether a depressing march, and, including those we shot, we passed fully 100 dead animals. The following account of the sufferings of animals in this campaign seems to me very realistic: "A horse drops wearily upon its knees, looks round dumbly on the wilderness of blackness, then turns its piteous eyes upwards towards the skies that seem so full of laughing loveliness, then, with a sob which is almost human in the intensity of its pathos, the tired head falls downwards, the limbs contract with spasmodic pain, then stiffen into rigidity; and one wonders, if the Eternal mocked that silent appeal from those great sad eyes—eyes that had neither part nor lot in the sin or sorrow of war, how shall a man dare look upwards for help when the bitterness of death draws nigh unto him? The grey lines above, on flank, and front, and rear, were with greedy speed converging to one point, until they flock in a horrid, struggling, fighting, revolting mass of beaks and feathers above the fallen steed. A soldier on the outer edge of the extended line swings his rifle with swift back-handed motion over his shoulder, and brings the butt amidst the crowd of carrion. The vultures hop with grotesque, ungainly motions from their prey, and stand with wings extended, and clawed feet apart, their necks outstretched and curved heads dripping slime and blood, a fitting setting amidst the black ruin of war. The charger now looks upwards from eyeless sockets; his gutted carcase, flattened into a shapeless streak, shrinks towards the earth, as if asking to be veiled from the laughter of the skies. But there is neither pity from above nor shelter from below as the red wave of war sweeps over the land. God grant that Merry England may never witness on her own green meadow-lands these sights and sounds which meet the eye and ear on African soil." Our rear company did not get into camp (Wolhuter's Kop) till 7.30 P.M., after a twenty-three mile march.

August 22.—Sudden changes in the orders. I am ordered to take all the force on to Pretoria with Lord Kitchener, except the two other infantry battalions, four guns, and some of the mounted infantry, who go north with Smith-Dorrien. We paraded 5.30 A.M., and marched through Commando Nek and along the pretty and fertile valley between the Magaliesburg and Witwatersberg to Rietvlei (eighteen miles).

WAITING THE ORDER TO DISMISS

To face p. 170

We complete our 1000 miles' trek to-day, and in the last fourteen days we have covered no less than 224 miles—an average of sixteen miles a day—and that includes one day's rest; so, omitting that, the average is over seventeen miles per marching day, a really fine performance.

August 23.—We marched at 6.15 A.M. to Pretoria, halting at Daspoort by Lord Roberts' order, as he wished to see us. At 2.45 we marched on, and he met us outside the town and rode with me a considerable distance, then trotted on and waited for us with his staff and Lady Roberts, in the big square, where we marched past him. He was very complimentary about all the battalion had done. We then marched on to our camp at Arcadia. Distance to-day fourteen miles.

CHAPTER XVI

LORD ALBEMARLE'S MOVEMENT

THE following extract from the diary of Lieut.-Colonel Lord Albemarle, who returned to Bank on 11th August with 300 men, and subsequently rejoined head-quarters at Pretoria, may be of interest:—

Bank, August 15*th.*—I had been lately receiving constant telegrams from the G.O.C. (General Barton) at Krugersdorp, urging me to keep a sharp look out for De Wet, and it has become evident that that personage has succeeded in eluding pursuit yet another time. I am, however, unable to do much, as I have no cavalry. On Wednesday last, late in the evening, I received a cypher telegram, the subject of which was the movements of De Wet, who was said to be at Heckpoort, some fifteen miles north of Bank. I at once put myself into communication with the Com-

LORD ALBEMARLE'S MOVEMENT 173

mandant at Welverdiend, eighteen miles west on the railway. Although, as I have said, I had no cavalry, it appeared necessary on this particular night to make an effort, and if possible to locate De Wet, even if we could not oppose him. I therefore turned out 150 men, taken equally from the C.I.V. and dismounted Colonials, 300 of whom have succeeded the Yorkshire Light Infantry and Camerons. The whole force was under the orders of Captain J. H. Smith, C.I.V. Their orders were to establish a series of detached posts along the line, and to patrol three or four miles out in the direction of Welverdiend, and to return to camp before dawn. The Commandant at Welverdiend arranged to send mounted patrols five or six miles in our direction. Our force started about 11.30 P.M., the Colonials leading. The hours of the night passed slowly enough, and I spent most of the time wandering about and listening, but never straying very far from the telegraph office. Before dawn the troops returned, and at 5 A.M. all the garrison stood to arms, a custom which I felt obliged to adhere to in case of an early morning attack   The next day proved a more eventful one for us, and, as will be seen presently, was one of considerable anxiety to me, inasmuch as the safety of so many men might depend upon my action. It was about 3 P.M. when I received a telegram from Welverdiend asking if a certain convoy had passed through Bank. I was looking out of the office window at the moment, and noticed a cavalry column moving quickly from north to south. I at first thought it might be part of the convoy referred to, but soon saw that they were moving too quickly, and that they were hardly likely to be British. They were about 3000 yards away, and appeared to number about 400. I could see that they had no waggons; only a few Cape carts, and a good many led horses. They were taking no precautions beyond having two scouts 100 yards in front and on the flanks, were in close formation, and whoever they were, there could be no doubt that they were aware of the absence of guns and cavalry at Bank. I at once had my three horses saddled, the only ones in camp, and despatched a sergeant and two

LORD ALBEMARLE'S MOVEMENT 175

men of the Colonials on them, with orders to reconnoitre and report to me. The little column had now crossed the railway and disappeared behind a ridge, towards the village of Blaawbank, about one and a half miles away. My scouts had not proceeded far when I saw them meet a horseman with a white flag, so, seeing that something was up, I sounded the "alert," and confined all Kaffirs and strangers in the place under a double guard. At this time all the men of the Colonial Division were employed on the train, loading up their things preparatory to going to Krugersdorp. In five minutes, where all had been bustle and confusion around the train, the scene quickly changed, and the troops were all installed in the elaborate trenches and prepared for an attack at any point. It was satisfactory to note how quickly the Colonials grasped the situation, and how soon keen interest took the place of the habitual callousness, which is the general outcome of long campaigning.

I ordered the train to be taken several hundred yards in the direction of Welverdiend, in order that the invalids in the hospital at Bank should be less liable to injury. The rear of the camp was protected by a bog. In less time than it has taken to write this, one of the scouts returned with the news that the white flag which had halted about a quarter of a mile from the advance trench, was the bearer of a summons from General Delarey to surrender.

The written message, which followed, ran thus :—

"To the Officer Commanding the British Troops,
"Bank Station.

"With this I give Your Honour notice that I am here with 400 Burghers and two Nordenfeldt maxims. In order to prevent bloodshed, I require that you surrender, together with your 'Burghers' (*sic*), unconditionally and immediately lay down the arms, and that the troops march in this direction. —Yours, &c.   J. DE LA REY.
"*Vecht Generaal.*"

I at once sent my verbal reply: "Let 'em all come," instructing the messenger to leave no doubt as to our absolute refusal. Fearing that they would cut the wires as they had crossed the railway, I telegraphed as shortly as possible to G.O.C., Krugersdorp: —" General De La Rey demands surrender. Stop. Refuse."

After waiting about half-an-hour, we had the satisfaction of seeing "the burghers trekking" towards the Gatsrand, but it was with sorrowful hearts that we reflected that a couple of guns or some mounted men might have placed De La Rey "in the palms of our hands." A little later I received two telegrams anxiously inquiring about the train, and when it would start; as it was impossible for me to tell whether the Boers were tapping the line, no answer was vouchsafed to them. Later on, however, I wired to the G.O.C. that the train would not start, at the same time directing that steam should be kept up until further orders. That night I sent out my three scouts in the direction taken by the Boers, and they reported that they had come upon a small covering party about a mile and a half away. It was a dark night. Several telegrams passed between Bank and Krugersdorp and Welverdiend, but I did not hear until the next morning that Broadwood's Cavalry Brigade and 400 infantry had been despatched to Bank. I also received a telegram from General Barton, "Hold on till I come." The cavalry arrived at mid-day, and exchanged much chaff with us over what they facetiously called "The relief of Bank Station." The C.I.V. officers at Bank were Captain Mortimore, Captain Smith, R.S.O., Messrs. Jeffrey, Greenwell, Gascoigne, and Haggard; Colour-Sergeant O'Connor was Acting Sergeant-Major. Where all ranks played up so well, it is impossible to say that one was more useful than another, but it was a great satisfaction to me that Captain Mortimore was Acting Adjutant, and Captain Smith R.S.O.

On the following morning, the people from the village of Blaawbank declared that De Wet had been seen by them, and that he was with Delarey, but I expect they were mistaken. One, Mrs. Roos, came with tears in her eyes to tell me that her husband and two horses had been carried off by the Boers.

LORD ALBEMARLE'S MOVEMENT

I, however, produced the spouse, and was the witness of an affecting domestic scene! On the Friday afternoon, we entertained General Broadwood, Tommy Brand, and Sudley to tea and tinned beef, and many officers of the Cavalry Brigade to tea and ration jam in a room about twelve foot square. Phipps Hornby, the new V.C., was one of those present; also Napier Miles, Longford, Fitzgerald, Barry, Fergusson, and Carter, all of the Household Cavalry, surnamed "Compos."

We left Bank on the 25th of August by train. At Krugersdorp we were joined by my brother-in-law, Leslie Davidson, R.A., Colonel on the Staff, who continued the journey with us as far as Johannesburg, where we parted. On arrival here, beyond the R.S.O., there was no Staff Officer to meet us, and no one to give us any orders. So I at once detrained, and leaving our impediments under a guard at the station, marched to the Agricultural Show Ground, which I understood was the most likely place for us to go to. Even now it was some time before I unearthed a Quartermaster-Sergeant, or any one who knew anything about us. I presently found the Colonel of the East Lancashire Battalion, who very kindly made all arrangements for us, half of my men bivouacking under a shed, and the remainder taking over the tents of the Yeomanry who were just leaving. The word "leaving" in this case was both active and neuter, for they left every kind of thing lying about in their tents; cartridges, spurs, straps, blankets, and even a saddle. In the evening, our baggage arrived in the waggons which I had requisitioned. We stayed here two days.

Johannesburg is a fine town in itself, fitted up according to the latest European pattern, with electric light, telephones, tram lines, smart clubs, large hotels with maple furniture and lifts, gaudy-looking villas, elegant public buildings, imposing hospitals and public gardens, racecourse, and agricultural show ground, but it is surrounded by an incongruous agglomeration of tin, mud, brick, and wooden buildings extending for many miles on every side, from which rises a veritable forest of tall chimneys emitting all the noxious gases and poisonous

C.I.V.'S SHEDDING TEARS (PEELING ONIONS)

Photo by Underwood & Underwood

To face p. 180

smoke common to a Wolverhampton or an Oldham. Even now, when the country is under the influence of a military occupation, the tradesmen who remain ply their trades, and the shop-fronts vie with one another in their efforts to display what remains to them of wares that have survived the grasping hand of the Dutch marauder. In monetary dealings no man speaks of a sixpence, and what is universally known as a Bob usurps the place of the more humble coin. In extraordinary circumstances, it is possible to obtain for £2 what in England would realise a third of that sum.

During my short stay here I dined with Tom Cochrane, to meet General Wavell. He lives in a very nice house, which belongs to a Dutchman. The ménage and cuisine are well ordered, and suitable for an officer of such importance as the provost-marshal of Johannesburg.

Our next move was to join the Colonial Division, four miles out, at Orange Grove, lately commanded by General Brabant, but now by Lieut.-Colonel Maxwell, R.E. On our arrival we found the mounted portion of the Division and four guns just starting on a three days' reconnaissance, so we might have been left in peace at the Agricultural Show Ground. As senior Lieut.-Colonel, I took over the command of the whole force from this date. We camped upon a nice piece of ground among some fir trees, with wood and water close at hand. The Colonial Division were most hospitable, and provided tents for the officers and men, and we subsequently found on the march that they had plenty of rum! As regards the safety of the camp, I was surprised to find the force encamped beneath a horseshoe-line of hills, which immediately overlooked it, and on another side was a thick fir wood, six hundred yards distant, which might harbour any amount of Boers. The only guard in the place was an examining guard on the road in the direction of Pretoria, and another in the nek leading to Johannesburg, who appeared to spend their time in the farmhouse. General Wavell had especially enjoined me to be very careful, as this locality, he said, was frequently visited by the enemy, so I thought it necessary to throw out a line of outposts on all sides, at the same time strengthening the examining guard and providing a cavalry patrol in the early morning. As this only entailed the employment of one hundred men per day, I did not consider it an excessive demand. On the day after our arrival, General Wavell and Tommy Cochrane came to tea with me, and the former entirely approved of the dispositions I had made. We remained here four days before starting out for Pretoria. The remainder of the Colonial Division returned on the evening of the third day. In order to make it as easy as possible for the infantry, I arranged to take three days marching to Pretoria, which we reached on Saturday, September 1. On arrival in sight of Klapper Kop, I helio'd the approach of the C.I.V. and Colonial Division to Six Mile Spruit, where we bivouacked for the night of Friday, August 31.

Before, however, crossing the spruit to take up our camping-ground, I directed half of the cavalry advance guard to occupy two kopjes which commanded the camp. Shortly afterwards they sent back hurriedly for the remaining half, as they reported seeing a party with a white flag in the plain below, and thought that these were a party of the enemy. I therefore sent back to Colonel Maxwell, directing him to be prepared for eventualities. After waiting some time, the news came that the party with the white flag were engineers working on the line, and that this was the way they protected themselves from possible attack. The next morning we continued our advance. Captain Mortimore rode on in front, according to orders from headquarters, to receive directions as to the disposition and distribution of the force on arrival at Pretoria. On arriving at a point about two miles from the town, I was met by a staff officer with the information that the Colonial Division was to return at once by road to Johannesburg, and that we ourselves were to go there by rail. I therefore took leave of our friends the Colonials and marched to the station at Pretoria, where I at once drew three days' tinned rations, and

LORD ALBEMARLE'S MOVEMENT

waited in the coal-yard till our train should be ready. I had a long conversation on the telephone with Colonel Ewart, who has now replaced Colonel Grierson at headquarters, and before leaving the instrument received fresh orders to join the rest of the C.I.V. at Das Poort, where they were encamped, some three miles to the north of Pretoria. After feeding the men, we proceeded on our journey, and without further incident rejoined the colours.

CHAPTER XVII

AT PRETORIA FOR THE THIRD TIME

[DE WET having escaped us, and his force having dispersed, the principal theatre of operations is now east of Pretoria, where the Boers are being slowly forced back along the Komati-Poort railway by Buller, Ian Hamilton, and Pole Carew.]

August 24.—I and Ted dined with Walter Bagot at his very nice house, which belongs to General Grobler.

A horrible day, with a furious dust-storm, as bad as any we have experienced in South Africa. Lord Roberts and headquarter staff left for Machadadorp. Went to see, and had long talks with, Generals Maxwell and Tucker. The former takes Orr on as acting private secretary.

August 25.—Some mails arrived, portions of

the accumulations of four weeks. We changed our camp to Hermanstadt, which is outside Daspoort, and is about two and a half miles from the centre of the town. Two guns of a mountain battery joined our force under Captain Llewellyn. Reid went to Cape Town yesterday to bring up hats, clothing, &c. Our mounted infantry are at Arcadia, which is fortunate, as there are many pay and promotion questions to settle. Orr amuses me by saying that the Governor of Pretoria told him that he was very nearly asking the C.I.V. to provide a hangman, as there seemed to be no trade for which we could not find a master! Kitchener promises to get up Albemarle and his detachment, and also our draft, as soon as possible. The rest of Smith-Dorrien's brigade arrived and went into camp on the racecourse. I fear we are no longer to remain with him. Orr and I dined with General Maxwell, meeting Mr. Fiddes, the Political Secretary.

I said a few words to the battalion to-day, explaining that as all our hard work had been done to the satisfaction of so many Generals, it would be superfluous for me to say much.

I told them how much I appreciated all they had done; that I felt deeply for them in all their hardships; that I earnestly trusted they would soon get home, and that Lord Roberts had told me how much he hoped the course of events might take them back to England before very long.

August 26.—Fitzclarence left us to join the 7th Fusiliers, in which he has got a commission. We furnished two companies to escort a convoy towards Commando Nek. Lady Roberts sent some tobacco and underwear for our men, accompanied by a note.

Armourer-Serjeant Gordon rejoined us with boots, &c., from Bloemfontein, having been to Bank *en route*, and from there he brought me an interesting letter from Albemarle,[1] telling how our detachment had been summoned to surrender by an impudent party of Boers. We send a guard of 100 men under Howell, Green, and Tyrwhitt to Government House; also twelve men go to-day to Lord Kitchener's, to act as cyclist orderlies—they are mounted on cycles taken from the Boers. I dined

[1] Extracts from this are given in Chap. XVI.

with Lord Kitchener, meeting Smith-Dorrien, Inglefield, and Fry (West Yorks).

August 27.—Gascoigne left us to-day to join his regiment—Seaforth Highlanders. It is sad to lose so many officers and men, but still it is for their own good, and it is a great thing for the regiment to get so many commissions in the regular army.

Ted and I called on Lady Roberts and had tea with her. We also went to see our Government House guard; the men looked smart, and are proud of their duty, to have been selected for which is a compliment to the regiment.

August 28.—Garnett rejoined from Germiston with forty convalescents. The draft of three officers and 106 men arrived, the officers being Captain Byrne, Lieutenant Selfe, and Lieutenant Carr. The men call them the "Volunteer Company."

August 29.—I inspected the draft, and was much pleased with the appearance of the men. The rainy season was heralded early this morning by a terrific thunderstorm; the lightning was splendidly vivid.

All the officers who made the big trek,

lunched with me at the Transvaal Hotel, and I got General Maxwell and Walter Bagot to meet them. We afterwards adjourned to the officers' guard-room, Government House, where we were all photographed. Greenwell joined us to-day from Bank, having come from Johannesburg by train.

August 30.—Lieutenant Glover rejoined us. He left us as a private at Winberg in medical charge of a convoy, and was afterwards given a lieutenant's commission.

August 31.—Henderson (cyclist) rejoined. He was taken prisoner outside Heilbron when carrying despatches, and was left sick by the Boers at Vredefort.

September 1.—The strength to-day of the battalion in South Africa is, excluding officers, 1043. On arrival in February it was 1049. Our casualties are 117, which include 28 deaths and 76 men invalided home; and against that, 111 men joined us in the draft, or rather arrived in South Africa in the draft. I lunched with our "Queen's Guard" to-day at the guard-room, Government House.

September 2.—We had church parade at nine,

PRETORIA FOR THE THIRD TIME 191

the first for seven weeks. I read the service, Ted taking the Lesson, and Jonah acting as precentor. The detachment under Albemarle marched in at 5 P.M., having come by road from Johannesburg.

September 3.—Mortimore, who has been gazetted to the Royal Artillery, left us to-day, very much to every one's regret.

Ted and I went up to the mounted infantry at Arcadia, where Cholmondeley wanted us to see some men. I saw the whole detachment, who looked fit, and were very responsive when I asked them if they wanted to go home. I gave two men their discharges on urgent private affairs, and heard a renewed application from Acting Sergeant-Major Rouse on the question of his rank being confirmed as sergeant-major, and from Prentice, the master-cook, also on the question of his pay. I promised in both these cases to ask for replies to former applications. We lunched there, and looked in at the "Queen's Guard" on our way home.

At eight to-night a sudden order came for 3 officers and 100 men to proceed to the railway station, and go north on an armoured train to repair the line near Warm Baths, where a train had been wrecked. Edis at once marched off with F. Company. A notice is published to-day that the Transvaal is annexed from 1st September.

Sorry to hear of the death of Private Thick, who was wounded at Frederickstadt; it was a nasty wound, the bullet going in on the right side of his stomach and travelling round his body to the spine, where it broke itself up in three pieces, which Sleman successfully extracted.

September 4.—A private letter from the Johannesburg Hospital says: "R. Streat, who was wounded at Frederickstadt, has won golden opinions here as a bright cheery lad. He has gone through a lot of pain, and no one has heard him utter a word of complaint."

Jonah and I dined with the Household Cavalry, and on our return found orders had come for us to move to-morrow morning to Proclamation Hill, about three miles from here.

September 5.—I gave Private Marden (E. Company) his discharge specially to-day, to

PRETORIA FOR THE THIRD TIME

enable him to take up employment on the railway at Johannesburg; he is a joiner, and his wages are to be 16s. 8d. a day. We changed our camp at 8 A.M., and relieved the 4th Battalion Derbyshire on Proclamation Hill, some three miles west of the railway station, sending D. Company to Eastern Redoubt, about eight miles on the other side of the city.

Ted and I went to the market, which was nearly empty. There are hardly any supplies in yet, except vegetables. Eggs are 7s. 6d. a dozen.

We then paid a short visit to the Museum, and rode on to our mounted infantry, where we dined and slept. They entertained us splendidly, and the concert after dinner was excellent; Jonah brought down the house with two topical songs. They had asked some forty nurses, mostly from the Langman and Welsh Hospitals, who looked picturesque in the moonlight, and who thoroughly enjoyed it. F. Company rejoined the battalion to-day.

September 6.—We had breakfast with the mounted infantry, then rode on to Eastern

Redoubt, where D. Company now are, then back to our camp, getting in at 1.30.

Matthey rejoined us to-day, having had an exciting time near Heidelberg, where his train was peppered with shots, but the plucky engine-driver put on full steam and ran the train into the station, though both he and the stoker were killed, the latter at once, the former dying of his wounds soon after getting in. Surely a gallant couple of men!

We took over to-day the tents of the Derbyshire Militia, and are once more under cover after having been for five months lying out in the open. Tents are not so welcome just now, as the weather is perfect, and the nights not at all cold. Saw Thorne of the Battery, who has come in rather seedy. C. Company proceeded to take up outpost duty on the Daspoort Range, about three miles north.

Sorry to hear of the death of Private Fraser Coombes, F. Company, whom I had specially sent to the Railway Department at Johannesburg, where he was employed in the Surveyor's Office. He was an architect by profession.

September 7.—Tyrwhitt, with fifty men, went off at 9 A.M. as escort to a traction engine convoy to Rietfontein. Weekes, who has got a commission in the West India Regiment, left us for England.

September 8.—Tyrwhitt returned with his escort. Reid came back from Cape Town, bringing some men and a great many welcome stores with him.

September 9.—Brigade church parade; only the Hampshires there with us. Parson somewhat conversational, prefacing the hymn with "I don't want this to be a solo, as I have four other services to-day." Our last hymn was sung to the tune of "'Home, sweet Home,' so that we can think of home while we are singing." Mr. Rose, who was our chaplain at Orange River, came up by request to hold a voluntary evening service, which was well attended. He gave a touching address, and dilated on the importance of keeping up our health and spirits in this time of "inaction and reaction."

September 10.—N.C.O.'s and men who are medically fit are slowly rejoining us, and our numbers are gradually increasing. Pom has a touch of fever, and has gone to the Irish Hospital; Arnold, too, is not very well, and slept in the town to-night.

September 11.—Pom and Arnold both better. Ted, Firth and I, accompanied by my orderly, Corporal Castle Smith, Sergeant Hall, and Colour-Sergeant Palmer, went to Johannesburg by train. Ted and I put up with Tom Cochrane, who is Acting Provost-Marshal. We dined at the Club, and saw Pawle, who seems happy in his new appointment.

We were shown over the Hospital in the Wanderers' Club grounds by Colonel Hamilton Large. It is beautifully laid out and appointed, and is the perfection of cleanliness and comfort. Saw some of our sick, including Bellairs, cyclist. After he was sent with his letter on the night of 14th August, his bicycle broke down hopelessly, so he deserted it, and walked close on fifty miles during the night. At daybreak, as he saw 300 Boers near him, he lay down in a swamp, with just his head showing. They moved away, and an hour later two mounted men came straight for him. He gave himself up for lost when, to his joy, he heard them speak English. They proved to be British Lancers, who took him to camp, and dried and fed him. But within a few hours pneumonia came on, and he went to hospital, where he has been very seriously ill for some weeks; he is now better, and was rejoiced to see us.

We looked over the Rontgen ray photos, and saw one very curious case, where two different bullets had lodged themselves in a man's arm, one immediately behind the other, but without touching one another, and each bullet was in a perfect state of preservation. We went to see our three cyclists, Mosley, Renshaw, and Thin, who are all doing good work. They live with three other legal luminaries in a house called the "C.I.V. mess," and are very comfortable.

September 12.—I felt quite strange, waking up inside sheets and in a room. Had a splendid bath and breakfast. This house, which is 63 Wolmarans, belongs to a Mr. Rissik, a Hollander, who is now a prisoner of war on parole. This is the fashionable quarter of the town, and the houses are beautifully furnished and well built.

We looked up many of our men who are employed here, and got leave for some of those who are *not* employed to return to the regiment. We lunched with Pawle at the station, and left at 2 P.M., arriving at Pretoria at 8, and in camp at 9.

September 13.—Arnold seedy again, with a temperature of 103°; he is wisely sleeping in the town. Sleman is also rather unwell.

September 14.—The sick officers are all improving. The weather is getting perceptibly better and the flies swarm. The news of Kruger's flight to Lorenço Marques is published. Green takes up the position of Railway Staff Officer to-day.

September 15.—Arnold went down to Cape Town. The change will do him good, and he will be useful to us in seeing to several things in connection with our embarkation.

September 16.—Pom went to Johannesburg for a change. We attended brigade church parade, service being conducted by a Canadian chaplain. Curious reminder of the size of the Empire, having Mr. Rose, an Australian, last Sunday, and a Canadian to-day!

1500 tins of tobacco arrived, a present from the Corporation of London, with best wishes. Cabled the thanks of the regiment home.

September 17.—G. Company returned to headquarters from the Queen's Guard, and were relieved by E. Company, Haggard remaining up there with Shipley.

September 18.—Fifteen of our men went to the Provost-Marshal to-day, in answer to a circular asking for permanent railway police, and eight of them are accepted at once; they begin work at Pretoria Station to-morrow. The mail of the 23rd June (!) arrived to-day; it has been travelling about in an ox-waggon for six weeks. Very sorry to hear that we have a case of cancer in the neck, and also a case of scarlet fever.

The principal medical officer inspected our camp to-day, and found everything very clean. Since the 15th we have been boiling all the drinking water, and the only thing that I can think of as being unhealthy is the smell of dead animals, which comes in rather strongly with a west wind.

September 19.—The terms of service for men with the Transvaal Police are published, and I asked for names of candidates. The pay is ten shillings a day, with free rations and board. Our convalescents who are north of Orange River are being called in to rejoin us by the Chief of the Staff, and they are gradually coming in.

September 20, 21, 22.—E. Company returned from "Queen's Guard" to headquarters, on relief by the Coldstream Guards. Lord Roberts inspected them before leaving Government House, and was very appreciative of their smartness and turn out. Later on I called on him, and found him, as usual, full of kind inquiries about the regiment. He promises to get us home as soon as the exigencies of the service will permit.

Ted and I went on to see our mounted infantry and D. Company, and then lunched with Kilkelly at the Yeomanry Hospital, afterwards going over the wards, stores, kitchens, &c.; it is beautifully arranged. Byrne, who has had slight fever, is in the Irish Hospital, but is going on well. I am sorry to hear that Sergeant Dawborn, who joined us with the draft, and who went to hospital with sunstroke, is dangerously ill.

September 23.—Heard of the death of Privates Welsby and Say, mounted infantry, both from enteric fever. We attended brigade church parade.

September 24.—Sergeant Dawborn died.

September 25.—I attended Sergeant Dawborn's funeral.

Lord Roberts sent for me at 6 P.M., and spoke to me about the regiment going home. Although, he said, it was not very convenient to spare them just now, still they had done so well that he was determined to let them go, as he knew how important their engagements were at home. He then asked me about dates, and finally said he would try to get the regiment off on Monday next. I rode back to camp and informed the battalion, and there was much cheering.

September 26.—Breakfasted with John Orr, and sent various cables about our impending departure. Ted and I rode over to see the mounted infantry and also D. Company.

September 28.—Had a "steady" drill. The men moved capitally, and the march past and manual exercise were first rate. Had the following telegram while on parade : " General Smith-Dorrien to Colonel MacKinnon.—I hear the C.I.V.'s. are about to return home, and it is a matter of sincere regret to me that I shall not see you all before you go. All good luck to yourself, Albemarle, Cholmondeley, and the whole of your gallant corps, and may we meet in England. No regiment in the army of South Africa has done more splendid work; and I have not only much appreciated the honour of having them under my command, but I have been given a pleasure which I shall never forget. Up to the last some of the corps have been with me, and to-day Concanon, Manisty, Henderson, fifty-six non-commissioned officers and men of the C.I.V. start from here to join you. This little band of mounted infantry have done, to my mind, the finest mounted infantry work I have seen this campaign. For three days they were our

PRETORIA FOR THE THIRD TIME

only mounted troops, the Boers disputing position after position with rifles and guns; but such was the dash and skill with which Concanon worked his men that our advance was not even delayed. Good-bye, and all the good luck they deserve to the C.I.V.'s."

I read this message to the battalion, who were deeply gratified, and, later, I replied: "C.I.V. regiment most grateful for kind message, which was read on parade. They will always remember with great joy the happy times spent under your command, and they sincerely wish you every success in the future."

The battery arrived, and encamped close to us, under the hill.

We gave an "At home" for Lord and Lady Roberts, and had a smart guard of honour under Howell to receive them. Our bleak kopje was much enlivened by the two or three carriages, the staff, and the escort. Shipley, mess president, gave us a capital tea, in which Sergeant Dunbar assisted him, and it was a great success. All our mounted infantry and battery officers came, and the men cheered vociferously as "Our Colonel" rode away.

September 29.—The beginning of our move. Triggs proceeded south with an advance party of 10 mounted infantry and 20 of the battalion. I lunched with Stanley, meeting Sir W. Nicholson and Wilson. Later, Stanley came out to see our camp, as also did Brabazon and Walter Bagot.

September 30.—Brigade church parade. An appropriate farewell sermon, and quite thirty of us attended holy communion, sitting on the veldt round a bell tent. Discharged a few men who wish to take up civil employment. Thirty convalescents arrived, many of them only just recovered from enteric. They are excused all duty, and Sleman takes extra care of them, giving them soup in the evening.

We returned all our transport, which has done good work, having been through the whole trek with us. Altogether we have been lucky with our native drivers, and I think they have had a happy time with the battalion. They all retire to their homes, having amassed a perfect fortune, for their pay has been £4, 10s. a month.

October 1.—Lunched with Ward, meeting

Duff and three or four others. Crabbe came in afterwards. Left P.P.C. cards on Lady Roberts and the Club. Our companies on detachment rejoined us.

Went round hospitals to say good-bye to those of our men unfit to accompany us. Found all doing well except Preuss, who, I fear, cannot live.

October 2.—Lord Roberts inspected the whole regiment on the ground underneath our camp, and made us a splendid speech, in which he dilated on the work we have done, told us how proud he was to be our Colonel, and ended up by saying, " One word more, men. When you arrive at home, give a thought to one who, although absent from you in body, will be present with you in spirit, and whose ambition it was, as your Colonel, to ride into London at your head."[1] It was an impressive parade, and after it was over I presented to Lord Roberts those officers of the regiment whom he had not seen before, and as he rode away we gave him three cheers. I afterwards spoke to the officers of the battalion, and thanked them

[1] See Appendix.

for all they had done during the eight and a half months I had been with them.

I rode up to Lord Roberts at 11 o'clock, at his request, to talk over the cases of men for civil employment whom we leave behind, and then on to the station, where I got into the 12.30 passenger train with the quartermaster, orderly-room clerk, all the pay sergeants, and a few others of the headquarters, so as to get to Cape Town before the regiment arrives, in order to discharge there the men who don't return to England, &c., &c. Byrne, who has been sick in the Irish Hospital, and John Orr, who has given up his appointment on the Government's staff, and who is also sick with dysentery, come with me. Sorry to hear just before I left of Preuss's death.

Our first troop train is to start at 3.30 P.M. with the battery, G. Company, and officers' horses; our second at 5 A.M. to-morrow with the mounted infantry; and the last two at 5.30 and at 6 to-morrow morning with the remainder of the battalion. We arrived at Vilgoen's Drift at 6.30 P.M., and stayed all night in the train, as more than one commando is in the neighbourhood.

TRANSPORT BY TRAIN

Photo by L. Green Wilkinson

To face p. 206

CHAPTER XVIII

HOME

October 3.—Left at 5 A.M., and arrived at Bloemfontein at 8 P.M. Left again at 9.

October 4.—Arrived at Norval's Pont at 7 A.M., and at Naauwpoort at 1 P.M., which we did not leave till 4. Colonel Du Cane offered us hospitality. We reached De Aar at 8, and left at 9. These two days travelling have been depressing ones, as we have continually come across wrecked trucks, burnt letters, the graves of soldiers, and the carcases of animals. One or other of these signs of war was in evidence almost every minute.

October 5.—Arrived at Beaufort West at 8.30 A.M. I met several friends, including Colonel Goldsmid, Captain Wilkinson, and also M'Culloch of the R.A. A fiendish sandstorm blowing, but had many luxuries as a compensation—butter, milk, and Bass's beer; also a good bath. Wilkinson was very attentive to us, and we transferred into the Cape mail, leaving at noon. The storm has disarranged the telegraph service, and as it is a single line, our train is much delayed. Stopped at Matjesfontein at 8 P.M.

October 6.—Arrived at Cape Town, 11.30 A.M. I jumped out amid a crowd of people into the arms of the Mayor (not having any idea he was there), and before I had found my legs, he had begun a speech of welcome. I made a short reply, the people cheered, and we drove off to the dock, and went on board the *Aurania*, where we found every arrangement being made for our comfort.

I went off to the Bank and various places, lunched with Currey at the Club, and spent the afternoon on board. Two of our cyclists asked me for leave to go ashore, and, when I inquired what they wanted leave for, they said, "We are asking Lord Justice Romer to dine, and perhaps you will come to meet him!" Dined with John Orr at the Mount Nelson Hotel. We looked in at Government House afterwards, and had a talk with the High Commissioner. The weather keeps cold and very wet.

October 7.—The first troop train arrived at 6 A.M. (the Battery and G. Company) and we at once began embarking. First, the men had coffee, then they handed in their old blankets and waterproof sheets (and very glad I was to get rid of them, as they had slept in them on the ground for eight months) and the ammunition into a shed, to be left behind; then the rifles and sidearms were taken on board, and the men returned on shore, to draw their sea-kits; after that, companies complete were marched on board to their respective "messes." The second train (infantry, under Bailey) arrived at 9 o'clock, and reported that Private Callingham had been jerked off one of the trucks up-country, and the train had gone right over him—a shocking thing, for the poor fellow had done all the trek, and was eagerly looking forward to getting home. The third train (mounted infantry) got in at 11 A.M., and the last (infantry, under Trotter) at

1 P.M. All the regiment were comfortably settled down by 3.

I had a cable from Lord Roberts, "Good-bye, and good luck to you all," to which I replied, "C.I.V. deeply grateful for their Colonel's telegram, and sincerely wish him, Lady Roberts, and the Misses Roberts an early and prosperous voyage home." A cablegram also came from the Lord Mayor, wishing us a pleasant journey.

At 1 o'clock, General Sir F. Walker came on board, and was much pleased with the appearance of the men and their smartness in embarking. At 4 o'clock the High Commissioner, Sir Alfred Milner, arrived, and was received with as much ceremony as we could command. We had a guard of honour of 100 men (though of course without arms) to line the gangway to the side of the ship. He came on board and made a short speech to the men, and before leaving inspected part of their quarters.

At five o'clock the order was given to let go, and, amid the cheers of the people, the great ship moved out of dock. It was smart work getting 1300 men detrained and embarked in so short a time, and the embarking staff officer told me he had never had a regiment so easy to manage.

It was cold and wet, and we found it very rough outside, with a north-west wind, not nearly half of us appearing at dinner.

October 8.—A great deal of motion during the night, but wind gradually fell. Run up to noon (eighteen hours) 248 miles.

October 9.—Fine and warm. Run 363 miles. Carter, Ted's servant, has got enteric, but is doing well.

October 10.—353 miles. Fine weather.

October 11.—358 miles. We have four cases of enteric and two of pneumonia, but they are all doing well. A concert to-night in the saloon.

October 12.—In the tropics. Weather muggy and cloudy. Run 356 miles.

October 13.—Same weather. Run 362 miles.

October 14.—Hotter. Church parade in the saloon, conducted by the Rev. S. E. Smith, who is on board, homeward bound.

Corporal Frapwell stripped himself to-day and showed me where he was hit by the bullet in the left shoulder-blade, and the point of exit, which was in front of the base of the stomach on the right side. A marvellous escape! Run 342 miles only, due to the bad coal. The sun is now to the south of us at noon. We are a week out to-day, and have not seen either land or a ship, nor, indeed, anything at all, except a whale and some flying-fish.

October 15.—Very hot, with the wind dead aft. Run 347 miles. We crossed the line.

October 16.—Poor Hutchins (C. Company) died of enteric at 1.30 this morning, and four hours later, just before daylight, we put the body into the sea. He was a splendid soldier, and his death is very sad, just as we are on our way home; he was sick before we left Pretoria, and there is no doubt his anxiety to get on board ship prevented his lying up sooner, as he ought to have done. He did all the marching with the battalion, and was also for a long time regimental policeman.

Run 352 miles. About noon the wind

shifted to the north-east, and we are now perceptibly cooler in the north-east trades.

October 17.—Run 333 miles.

October 18.—Run 318 miles. At 3 P.M. we sighted the island of Sant Iago. It is wonderful to think that, after our voyage of 3800 miles out of sight of land, the land should appear in the exact direction expected.

October 19.—Arrived at St. Vincent at 6 A.M., found many cablegrams, including one of 200 words, giving the programme of our reception in London. The Governor of Cape Verde Islands paid me an official visit at 2 P.M. We had a guard of honour for him, and entertained him with champagne. He invited us to a ball at the new hospital.

Tom Cochrane heard of his election to Parliament.

Forty of us went to the ball at 9 P.M. It was very well done, and the Portuguese Staff were most hospitable. In the opening square dance my partner was the Governor's secretary's wife, who spoke neither English nor French. I spoke to her very fluently in

French (her ignorance of it gave me great confidence), and she kept on turning round to her husband, who stood behind her, and shrugging her shoulders. So at last I "took on" the husband instead, while Madame stood aloof, and the end of our dance was not very sociable. The last of the officers got back on board at 2 A.M.

As the London authorities are anxious for us to arrive on Friday at Southampton, every effort is being made to coal the ship quickly.

Poor Cameron (F. Company) died of enteric fever. This was the second attack of it he had had—a very rare occurrence.

October 20.—At six o'clock we weighed anchor and proceeded. I wrote a warm letter of thanks to the Governor for his hospitality, for I discovered that the King of Portugal had ordered every attention to be paid us, and the Governor had come 140 miles to meet us.

The *Britannia* is in harbour, and our captain is pleased that we beat her from Cape Town by a good many hours.

Soon after getting clear of land we buried Private Cameron. The poor fellow was useful to me with clerical work on the formation of the regiment last January. At 10 A.M. we met a large Italian steamer headed for St. Vincent, on fire. We turned round and followed her, but, as she signalled "Shall not abandon ship," we resumed our course.

Run up to noon 67 miles.

October 21.—Divine service as usual. Run 333 miles; very disappointing.

Poor Aylen (F. Company) died at 3 P.M. of enteric, and we had the funeral at 6 P.M.

October 22.—Run 330 miles; again disappointing.

October 23.—We were off Madeira at 10 A.M. Had a consultation with the captain as to whether to continue direct or to run to Funchal and cable that we could not arrive in England before Sunday. On the whole, captain inclined to keeping on. We have a fresh head-breeze. Had a concert to-night.

October 24.—Run only 292 miles. A heavy head-sea last night and this morning accounted for this.

October 25.—Run 306 miles. Strong north-east wind. I made up a return to-day showing that the total number of C.I.V.'s serving in South Africa has been 64 officers and 1675 other ranks. Of these there have been:—

	Officers.	Other ranks.	Total.
Killed and died	1	57	58
Wounded	1	60	61
Invalided home	5	151	156
Sick (S.A.)	—	48	48
Govt. Employ, &c. (S.A.)	2	119	121
Resigned	1	—	1
Given commissions	6	25	31
On board	48	1277	1325
Leave in England	2	—	2
	65	1677	1742[1]

One officer and two men are shown twice in the above, having been given commissions, and also being on board this ship.

Issued a farewell regimental order to-day as follows:—

"The Commandant wishes to impress on the N.C.O.'s and men the importance of marching through the streets of London in a soldier-like manner and of preserving to the last moment that strict sense of discipline which has been such a feature in the regiment.

[1] Wounded not added in total.

"There are no greater temptations to a soldier than when he returns home after a campaign; but as the City Imperial Volunteers have earned their reputation under trying circumstances, so the Commandant is sure that they will maintain it under trying circumstances to the end.

"He takes this opportunity of thanking the officers, N.C.O.'s, and men for the support they have given him and the cheerful and soldier-like feeling they have always shown; and while he regrets the time for breaking up the Corps has arrived, he congratulates all ranks on their return home, and wishes them health and prosperity in future."

I was awoke at 11.30 by Thorne reporting the sudden death of Private Bruce from heart failure; he had been suffering from enteric.

October 26.—Held the funeral at 7 A.M., all F. Company attending. Run 337 miles.

Weather, which has been changeable, culminates to-day in a north-west gale, which makes a very heavy beam-sea, and the ship rolls a great deal. Sighted Ushant at 9.30 P.M.

October 27.—Very bad night. Off the Start

at 8.30 A.M. Were welcomed by numerous steamers as we passed up Channel. Through the Needles at 3 P.M., and anchored off Netley Hospital at 4.

A great many telegrams and letters awaiting us, including one from Lord Roberts: "I congratulate C.I.V.'s on safe arrival. I feel no words of mine can add to the warm welcome they richly deserve, and will undoubtedly receive, from their fellow-citizens." Albemarle came off, surrounded by numerous reporters, &c.

October 28.—Church parade on board. Very wet day. No civilians allowed on the ship, and no men allowed, nor indeed did they apply to go, on shore.

October 29.—Poor Weston died at 4 A.M. His mother had come on board overnight, and was present with him, as also was his father. We came alongside the Empress Dock at 8 A.M., and began disembarking at 8.15.

The following message was received from Her Majesty the Queen: "The Queen is glad to hear of the safe arrival of the *Aurania*, trusts all on board are well, and wishes to know what kind of passage they have had."

We moved to London in four trains, travelling *viâ* Basingstoke to Paddington, whence we marched at 1.30 P.M. through crowds of people to St. Paul's, where a Thanksgiving Service was held; then on to the Guildhall, where we were formally welcomed by the Corporation; finally we arrived at Finsbury Barracks at 7 P.M., where the men handed in rifles and sidearms, and a banquet was given to us.

The men behaved admirably, not only when marching through the streets but after everything was over, and furloughs to the end of November were given to all ranks.

APPENDICES

APPENDIX A

ANALYSIS OF TRADES OF MEN IN CITY IMPERIAL VOLUNTEERS

OUT of 1260 men, the average age was 24 years; height, 5 feet 8 inches.

Religions were :—

Church of England	1126	Jews	16
Wesleyans	20	Baptists	5
Roman Catholics	32	Protestants	13
Presbyterians	35	Methodists	4
Congregationalists	3	Unitarians	3

Among the Trades were found :—

- 1 Queen's Foreign Office Messenger.
- 2 Bankers.
- 1 Shipowner.
- 9 Barristers.
- 1 Crown Law Officer.
- 2 Artists.
- 3 Surgeons.
- 4 Dental Surgeons.
- 1 Veterinary Surgeon.
- 2 House of Commons Clerks.
- 9 Law Students.
- 14 Stock Exchange.
- 16 Solicitors.
- 5 Writers to the Signet.
- 6 Secretaries.
- 7 Students.

APPENDIX

- 16 Surveyors.
- 29 Bank Clerks (about 12 from Bank of England).
- 308 Clerks.
- 30 Civil Service Clerks.
- 7 Architects.
- 6 Auctioneers.
- 3 Medical Students.
- 1 Distiller.
- 9 Jewellers.
- 4 Chemists.
- 1 Librarian.
- 4 Schoolmasters.
- 2 Analysts.
- 6 Accountants.
- 7 Farmers.
- 3 Hop Factors.
- 2 Hospital Attendants.
- 25 Independent (no business).
- 6 Insurance Brokers.
- 1 Metallurgist.
- 3 Photographers.
- 1 Timber Merchant.
- 5 Victuallers.
- 20 Printers.
- 37 Engineers.
- 1 Marine Engineer.

In addition to these, there were no less than 142 trades represented, including :—

- 48 Warehousemen.
- 23 Salesmen.
- 42 Carpenters.
- 38 Labourers.
- 14 Builders.
- 10 Post-Office Employés.
- 23 Plumbers.
- 13 Tailors.

And amongst the others an occasional :—

- Engine-Driver.
- Omnibus-Driver.
- Florist.
- Glass-Worker.
- Mosaic-Worker.
- Music Engraver.
- Perfumery Manager.
- Police Constable.
- Pianomaker.
- Tax Surveyor.
- Varnish Tester.
- Pawnbroker.
- Watch-Jobber.

APPENDIX B

Infantry Battalion C.I.V.—*State of Various Detachments comprising the above Battalion, 30th May 1890.*

Name of Corps.	Number (1) landed in S. Africa.	Number (2) now absent Sick.	Percentage of Column 2 to Column 1.	Number absent on Duty.	Other Causes.	Present at Headquarters.	Remarks.
1st London V.R.C.	37	5	13	15	...	17	
26th Middlesex	7	1	14	1	...	5	
2nd S. Middlesex	18	2	11	2	...	14	
24th Middlesex	7	1	14	3	...	3	
12th Middlesex	34	2	5	...	...	32	
K.R.R. Cadets	15	4	26	...	...	11	
Hon. Art. Com.	18	5	27	2	...	11	
1st V.B. Middlesex	36	10	27	3	2	21	
2nd V.B. Middlesex	32	8	25	1	...	23	
17th Middlesex	20	1	5	...	5	14	
18th Middlesex	24	3	12	1	...	20	
1st L.V.R.E.	14	6	42	1	...	7	
1st Middlesex R.E.	4	2	50	...	...	2	
5th Middlesex	31	8	26	...	...	23	
1st Surrey Rifles	13	3	23	...	...	10	
2nd E. Surrey Rifles	14	5	25	1	...	8	
3rd ,, ,,	39	6	15	...	...	33	
4th ,, ,,	24	5	20	...	...	19	
1st V.B. Queen's	12	2	16	...	...	10	
2nd ,, ,,	21	3	14	3	...	15	
3rd ,, ,,	18	3	16	...	2	13	
4th ,, ,,	26	3	11	1	...	22	
4th Middlesex R.V.	5	1	20	...	...	4	
22nd ,, ,,	21	2	9	...	1	18	
20th ,, ,,	58	7	12	1	...	50	
7th ,, ,,	31	6	19	2	...	23	
13th ,, ,,	29	2	7	2	1	24	
19th ,, ,,	29	6	20	4	...	19	
1st Victoria Rifles	31	7	22	1	...	23	
1st V.B. Essex	28	7	25	1	...	20	
2nd ,, ,,	25	3	12	...	1	21	
3rd ,, ,,	19	3	16	...	2	14	
4th ,, ,,	17	3	17	...	...	14	
1st V.B. Royal Fus.	11	...	Nil	...	...	11	
2nd ,, ,, ,,	8	2	25	...	...	6	
3rd ,, ,, ,,	27	7	25	...	...	20	
15th Middlesex	11	33	27	...	1	7	
21st Middlesex	44	19	43	...	...	25	
1st City of Lond. Art.	10	1	10	1	...	8	
1st Sussex Art.	14	5	35	...	...	9	
2nd Middlesex Art.	13	2	15	...	1	10	
2nd Kent Art.	4	...	Nil	...	...	4	
2nd London	33	15	45	...	1	17	
3rd London	25	7	28	1	...	17	
1st Tower Hamlets	24	6	25	1	1	16	
2nd Tower Hamlets	5	2	40	...	...	3	
16th Middlesex	25	9	36	...	2	14	
Total	1011	213	...	48	20	730	

APPENDIX C

FAREWELL ADDRESS TO THE CITY IMPERIAL VOLUNTEERS

PRETORIA, 2nd October 1900.

I COULD not allow you to leave Pretoria without wishing you good-bye and God-speed on your homeward journey.

I am glad you are going home, because you have well earned a holiday; but I am more sorry than I can say to lose you from this command, and I greatly regret that your early departure precludes me from the honour and pleasure, to which I have been looking forward for some months past, of marching, as your Honorary Colonel, at your head into London, and being with you when you receive that richly deserved tribute of admiration which will undoubtedly be offered to you by your fellow-citizens.

Statistics are dull things, but I think I must quote a few to you, as they will give your fellow-soldiers out here, and your fellow-citizens at home, some idea of what you have gone through in the service of your Queen and country.

Your total strength when you landed in this country was 1729 of all ranks, including the battery, the mounted infantry, and the battalion. Of these, 9 have been killed, 43 have died, 53 have been wounded, and 141 have been invalided; a total of 246, or slightly over 13 per cent.

You left the railway at Springfontein on the 16th April, and arrived at Pretoria for the third time on the 23d August. During these four months you marched on 75

APPENDIX

days, and covered a distance of 1018 miles—an average of 13½ miles a day—a fine performance, of which any regiment might well be proud, more especially a corps such as yours, drawn as it was from various sources, and composed of men not trained for war.

You are going home in advance of the other troops, because I feel that some consideration is due to those of you who have given up professions, situations, and employments to take your place in the ranks of Her Majesty's army; and that some consideration is due also to those employers who, through motives of patriotism, are keeping your places open until you return.

I have always been a firm believer in the Volunteer movement, and have had strong convictions that some of the best material in the army is to be found in our Volunteer force. Some few years ago, when I was Commander-in-Chief in India, an expedition was being prepared for service on the eastern frontier of Bengal, and I strongly recommended an application submitted by the Calcutta Volunteers that a company of that battalion might take part in the expedition. This was agreed to by the Government of India, and the company did excellent service on that occasion. The admirable work now performed by the C.I.V., the Volunteers attached to the regular battalions serving in South Africa, and the Imperial Yeomanry, have, I rejoice to say, proved that I was right, and that England, relying as she does on the patriotic Volunteer system for her defence, is resting on no broken reed.

You have proved your worth, and now you return to your homes to receive the well-merited applause of your fellow-countrymen, and I think I may say, without fear of making a mistake, of your countrywomen also.

But your work will not then be quite finished. You were drawn, I understand, from 53 Volunteer battalions. To each of these the men returning home will prove a tower of strength. You will be able to tell your comrades what war is like, and instruct them as to the manner in which they must prepare themselves for service in the field. And there is one other thing you can do; that is, to carry into the heart of the nation what you now know of the British soldier with whom you have fought shoulder to shoulder for some months past. Tell every one of his bravery, his endurance, his gentleness, and his good behaviour; tell them what a noble fellow he is, and how, at a moment's notice, he is prepared to lay down his life for his Queen and country.

One word in conclusion. When you march through the streets of London, give a thought of one man, who, though absent in person, will be present in spirit—your Honorary Colonel—who will ever remember with pride his connection with the corps which has brought honour to itself, and done such splendid service for Queen and country.

ROBERTS, *Field-Marshal*.

APPENDIX D

The battalion has passed the night at 97 different places in South Africa. Out of this time, there were no less than 59 changes of camp in the 80 days between 16th April (the day of leaving Springfontein) and the 5th July (the day of arrival at Heilbron).

The following is the list of camps. Board ship is counted as one, as also is each night in the train.

Feb.	15. On board ship.	Apl.	23. Bloemfontein.
,,	16. Green Point.	,,	25. Glen.
,,	20. Train.	,,	29. Kleinospruit.
,,	21. ,,	,,	30. Os-Spruit.
,,	22. ,,	May	1. Jacobsrust.
,,	23. Orange River.	,,	2. Isabellafontein.
,,	27. De Aar.	,,	4. The Wet Spruit.
Mar.	2. Train.	,,	5. Winburg.
,,	3. Orange River.	,,	8. Dankbaarsfontein.
,,	31. Train.	,,	9. Bloomeplatz.
Apl.	1. Naauwpoort.	,,	10. Zand River.
,,	10. Norval's Pont.	,,	11. Deelfontein.
,,	11. Springfontein.	,,	12. Kroonstad.
,,	16. Kuilfontein.	,,	15. Kronspruit Zuid.
,,	17. Jagersfontein.	,,	16. 13 miles E. of do.
,,	18. Kruger's Siding.	,,	17. Near Valsch River.
,,	19. Edenburg.	,,	18. Lindley.
,,	20. Bethanie.	,,	20. Koroospruit.
,,	21. Kaffir River.	,,	21. Vecht Kop.
,,	22. Kaals Spruit.	,,	22. Heilbron.

APPENDIX

May 23. Spitz Kop.
„ 24. Vredepoort.
„ 25. Marseilles.
„ 26. Vaal River.
„ 27. Wildebeestefontein.
„ 28. Syperfontein.
„ 29. Doorn Kop.
„ 30. Florida.
June 1. Johannesburg.
„ 3. Luckshai River.
„ 4. Zesmyl Spruit.
„ 5. Pretoria.
„ 6. Irene.
„ 8. Garsfontein.
„ 11. Donkershoek.
„ 12. Diamond Hill.
„ 13. Elands River.
„ 15. Schwartz Kop.
„ 16. Pretoria.
„ 19. Irene.
„ 20. Reitfontein.
„ 21. Springs.
„ 22. Bultfontein.
„ 23. Heidelberg
„ 27. Zukersboschrand River.
„ 28. Bierlaagte.
„ 29. Villiersdorp.
„ 30. Bankplaatz.
July 1. Frankfort.
July 4. Twelve-mile Spruit.
„ 5. Heilbron.
„ 24. Train.
„ 25. Krugersdorp.
„ 28. Bank.
„ 29. Wonderfontein.
„ 30. Frederichstadt.
Aug. 8. Welverdiend.
„ 9. Bank.
„ 10. Cherholzer.
„ 11. Welverdiend.
„ 12. Rietvlei (Mooi River).
„ 13. Zwart Kop.
„ 14. Syperwater.
„ 15. Leeuwfontein.
„ 16. Brakfontein.
„ 18. Tweirivier.
„ 19. Rustenburg.
„ 20. Hoedsspruit.
„ 21. Wolhuter's Kop.
„ 22. Rietvlei.
„ 23. Pretoria (Arcadia).
„ 25. „ (Hermanstadt).
Sept. 5. Pretoria (Proclamation Hill).
Oct. 2. Train
„ 3. „
„ 4. „
„ 7. On board ship.

APPENDIX E

NUMBER OF COURTS-MARTIAL IN THE C.I.V. REGIMENT DURING THE CAMPAIGN

Six courts-martial have been held—

- 2 for being asleep on sentry.
- 2 for theft.
- 1 for striking a sentry.
- 1 for absence.

Two of above were acquitted.

The sentences varied from 28 to 14 days' field imprisonment.

In one case, the whole 28 days were remitted, in consequence of the good behaviour of the regiment.

There have been 36 cases of imprisonment by commanding officer, 3 of which were for drunkenness, and nearly all the remainder for speaking improperly to non-commissioned officers.

APPENDIX F

RETURN OF 99 CASES OF ENTERIC FEVER CONTRACTED ON SERVICE IN SOUTH AFRICA, FEBRUARY TO OCTOBER 1900

Inoculated.

No. of Cases.	Deaths.	Percentage.
60	9	15.00

Non-inoculated.

No. of Cases.	Deaths.	Percentage.
39	11	28.20

Corrected to 15th October 1900.

R. R. SLEMAN, *Surgeon-Major, C.I.V.*

APPENDIX G

RETURN OF 104 CASES OF ENTERIC FEVER CONTRACTED ON SERVICE IN SOUTH AFRICA, FEBRUARY TO NOVEMBER 1, 1900, INCLUDING THOSE WHICH OCCURRED ON THE HOMEWARD VOYAGE

Inoculated.

No. of Cases.	Deaths.	Percentage.
65	18	27.69

Non-inoculated.

No. of Cases.	Deaths.	Percentage.
39	12	30.76

Corrected to November 1.

R. R. SLEMAN, *Surgeon-Major, C.I.V.*

APPENDIX H

THE CITY OF LONDON IMPERIAL VOLUNTEERS

Headquarters—GUILDHALL, LONDON, E.C.

Hon. Colonel.

F.C. ROBERTS, Field-Marshal, Rt. Hon. *F.S.*, Lord,
K.P., G.C.B., G.C.S.I., G.C.I.E., Col. Commandt.
R. Art. (R) *s.* . . . . 10th Mar. 1900

Colonel Commandant (Colonel on the Staff).

MACKINNON, Col. W. H. . . . . . 22nd Dec. 1899

Staff Captains.

TROTTER, Lt. E. H., G. Gds. (*temp. Capt. in Army*,
1st Jan. 1900). . . . . 1st Jan. 1900
ORR, J. E. H., late Lt. R. Art. (*temp. Capt. in Army*,
3rd Jan. 1900, *for Transport Duties*) . . . 3rd Jan. 1900

Depôt Commandant.

BOXALL, Hon. Col. C. G., C.B., 1 Suss. V.A.C. (*temp.
Lt.-Col. in Army*, 7th Feb. 1900 . . . 7th Feb. 1900

Depôt Adjutant.

GRANTHAM, Lt. W. W., 14 Middlesex V.R.C. (*temp.
Capt. in Army*, 10th March 1900) . . . 10th Mar. 1900

Medical Officer.

SLEMAN, Surg.-Capt. R. R., 20 Midd'x V.R.C. (*temp.
Capt.*, 9th Jan. 1900) . . . . . . 9th Jan. 1900

Paymaster.

TRIGGS, Capt. W., Res. of Off. . . . . . 10th Jan. 1900

Veterinary Surgeon.

MULVEY, W. S. (*temp. Vety.-Lt.*, 8th Jan. 1900) . 8th Jan. 1900

APPENDIX

FIELD BATTERY.

Major—with temporary rank of Major in Army.

McMicking, Major G., Honourable Artillery Company . . 8th Jan. 1900

Captain.

Budworth, Captain C. E. D., Royal Artillery . . . . 12th Jan. 1900

Lieutenants (3)—with temporary rank of Lieutenant in Army.

Lowe, Lieut. A. C., Honourable Artillery Company . . . 8th Jan. 1900
Bayley, Lieut. H., Honourable Artillery Company . . . 12th Jan. 1900
Duncan, 2nd Lieut. J. F., Honourable Artillery Company . . 12th Jan. 1900

Medical Officer—with temporary rank of Captain.

Thorne, Surgeon-Captain A., M.B., 2nd Middlesex V.A. . . 12th Jan. 1900

Veterinary Surgeon—with temporary rank of Veterinary-Lieutenant.

Morgan, E. . . . . 7th Feb. 1900

MACHINE GUN SECTION.

Lieutenant—with temporary rank of Lieutenant in Army.

Welby, Lieut. E. V., 1st Tower Hamlets V.R.C. . . . 8th Jan. 1900

MOUNTED INFANTRY.

Lieutenant-Colonel—with temporary rank of Lieutenant-Colonel in Army.

Cholmondeley, Hon. Colonel H. C., Lieut.-Col. Commandant
1st London V.R.C. . . . . 27th Dec. 1899

Captains (2)—with temporary rank of Captain in Army.

Waterlow, Captain J. F., 2nd V.B. Royal West Surrey Regiment 3rd Jan. 1900
Reid, Captain J. W., 3rd Middlesex V.A.C. . . . . 3rd Jan. 1900

Lieutenants (8)—with temporary rank of Lieutenant in Army.

Wilson, Captain C. H. W., 2nd V.B. East York Regiment . 3rd Jan. 1900
Concannon, Captain E. G., 16th Middlesex V.R.C. . . . 3rd Jan. 1900
Brailey, Capt. W. H., 3rd V.B.R. W. Surrey Regt. . . . 3rd Jan. 1900
Moeller, Lieut. B., Honorary Artillery Company, *c*.[a] . . 3rd Jan. 1900
Berry, Second Lieut. G., 13th Middlesex V.R.C. . . . 3rd Jan. 1900
Manisty, E. A. . . . . 3rd Jan. 1900
Henderson, Lieut. A. H., 21st Middlesex V.R.C. . . . 8th Jan. 1900
Baillie, D. G., *c*.[b] . . . . 18th Feb. 1900

Adjutant.

Bell, Capt. E., Worcester Regiment . . . . . . 10th Jan. 1900

---

[a] *2nd Batt. Middlesex Regt.* [b] *From the ranks.*

APPENDIX 233

Quarter-Master.

Ridler, Hon. Lieut. J., Riding-Master A.S. Corps . . . 6th Jan. 1900

INFANTRY.

Lieutenant-Colonel—with temporary rank of Lieutenant-Colonel in Army.

Albemarle, Hon. Colonel A. A. C., Earl of, Lieutenant-Colonel
12th Middlesex V.R.C. . . . . 3rd Jan. 1900

Second in Command with temporary rank of Major in Army.

Pawle, Hon. Colonel A. G., Lieut.-Colonel 18th Middlesex
V.R.C. . . . . 3rd Jan. 1900

Captains (8)—with temporary rank of Captain in Army.

Reid, Captain A., 1st V.B. Middlesex Regiment	3rd Jan. 1900
Berkeley, Captain C. W., 3rd London V.R.C.	3rd Jan. 1900
Matthey, Captain C. G. R., 1st London V.R.C.	3rd Jan. 1900
Cousens, Captain F. J., 5th Middlesex V.R.C.	3rd Jan. 1900
Shipley, Captain R. B., 1st Middlesex V.R.C.	3rd Jan. 1900
Edis, Hon. Major R. W. H., Captain 20th Middlesex V.R.C.	3rd Jan. 1900
Howell, Captain A. A., 3rd V.B. Royal Fusiliers	3rd Jan. 1900
Mortimore, Captain C. A., 3rd V.B. Royal West Surrey Regt., c.[a]	3rd Jan. 1900

Lieutenants (16) —with temporary rank of Lieutenant in Army.

Smith, Captain J. H., 5th Middlesex V.R.C.	3rd Jan. 1900
Benson, Captain J. P., 4th V.B. Essex Regiment	3rd Jan. 1900
Burnside, Captain W. F., 3rd V.B. East Surrey Regiment, c.[b]	3rd Jan. 1900
Jeffery, Captain F. R., 1st Surrey V.R.C.	3rd Jan. 1900
Alt, Captain W. B. L., 22nd Middlesex V.R.C., d.[1]	3rd Jan. 1900
Treffry, Lieutenant E., Honourable Artillery Company	3rd Jan. 1900
Townroe, Lieutenant E. D., 4th V.B. East Surrey Regiment	3rd Jan. 1900
McDonnell, Lieutenant Hon. S. K., C.B., 1st London V.R.C.	3rd Jan. 1900
Browne, Lieutenant P. F., 13th Middlesex V.R.C., c.[c]	3rd Jan. 1900
Garnett, Lieutenant W. B., 24th Middlesex V.R.C., c[d]	3rd Jan. 1900
Grindle, Lieutenant C. P., 19th Middlesex V.R.C.	3rd Jan. 1900
Green, Lieutenant B. C., 7th Middlesex V.R.C.	3rd Jan. 1900
Croft, Second Lieutenant P., 20th Middlesex V.R.C., c.[e]	3rd Jan. 1900
Hole, S. H. F.	3rd Jan. 1900
Cohen, Lieutenant J. W., 13th Middlesex V.R.C.	8th Jan. 1900
Marsh, Captain F. P., 1st V.B. Essex Regiment.	11th Jan. 1900

Adjutant.

Bailey, Captain Hon. J. H. R., Grenadier Guards . . . 9th Jan. 1900

Medical Officer—with temporary rank of Captain.

Ryan, Surgeon-Captain E. W. St. V., 16th Middlesex V.R.C. . 6th Jan. 1900

Quarter-Master.

Firth, Hon. Captain S., Quarter-Master Royal Artillery . . 6th Jan. 1900

---

[1] *Memorial not yet settled.*
[a] *R.G.A.* [b] *3rd Hussars.* [c] *Warwickshire Regiment.* [d] *R. Welsh Fusiliers.*
[e] *A.S.C.*

APPENDIX

LIST OF N.C.O.'S AND MEN OF THE REGIMENT[1] WHEN FIRST FORMED

d. after the name of any man indicates that he died; to all such names is appended a note stating the place where a Memorial has been erected.

c. after a man's name indicates that the man was given a Commission; the regiment to which he was gazetted is in each case appended in a note.

STAFF N.C.O.'s.

Rank.	Name.	Rank.	Name.
Sergt.-Major	Smith, T.	Sergt. Drummer	M'Nally, J. C.
,, ,,	Pilbrow, G. E.	Armourer Sergt.	Gordon, E. A. H.
,, ,,	Rouse, A. W.	Sergt. Pioneer	Taylor, E.
Qr.-Master-Sergt.	Donn, F.	Sergt. Cook	Prentice, S.
,, ,,	Oakley, P.	,, ,,	M'Govern, J.
Ord. Q.-M.-Sergt.	Hall, H. F.	Signalling Sergt.	Hutchison, J. T.
Orderly Rm. Clerk	Barter, E. B.	Transport Sergt.	Macfarlane, W.

ABBISS, P. J., 22nd Middlesex R.V.
Abrahams, A. G. W., 1st C. of Lon. Rifles
Abraham, F., H.A.C., Sergt.
Adams, P. E., 1st Lond. R.E., Corp.
Ager, F. G., 12th Middlesex R.V., Sergt.
Aimer, J., 3rd City of London Rifles
Airey, W. M., 7th Middlesex R.V.
Aiton, H. J., 3rd V.B.R. West Surrey
Alder, E. J., 3rd V.B. Royal Fus., Sergt.
Allen, C. G., H.A.C., L.-Corp.
Altass, F. C., 3rd V.B. R. West Surrey
Anderson, D. S., 1st London R.E.
Anderson, G. G., 13th Middlesex R.V.
Anderson, W. J., 3rd V.B. E. Surrey Rgt.
Andrews, H. W., 3rd Middlesex V.A.
Applebee, H. P., H.A.C.
Appleford, J. C., 13th Middsex. R.V., *d.*[2]
Archbald, J. F., 3rd V.B. Royal Fusil.
Archer, B. D.W., H.A.C., L.-Corp.
Argent, H. T., 2nd V.B. Essex Regimt.
Armstrong, C. R., 20th Middlesex R.V.
Armstrong, T. P. H., H.A.C.
Arnell, W. R., 5th Middlesex R.V.
Arnold, E. H., 17th (N.) Middsx. R.V.
Arnold, F. G., 3rd Middlesex V.A.
Arnold, W., 1st V. B. R. W. Surrey Rgt.
Ascott, J. A., 2nd V.B. Essex Regimt.
Atkins, W. H., 3rd Mx. V. A., Lce.-Cpl.
Atkinson, E. L., 1st Sur. R., Sergt., *d.*[3]
Attneave, H., H.A.C.,

Austen, E. E., 20th Midx. R.V., L.-Sergt.
Austin, F. C., 20th Middx. R.V., Corp.
Austin, J. M. C., 20th Mx. R.V., Col.-S.
Avern, H., 19th Middlesex R.V.
Aylen, F. N., 13th Middlesex R.V., *d.*[4]
Ayres, C. R., 1st Tower Hamlets R.V.

BAILEY, F. C., 1st C. of Lon. Artillery
Bailey, F. F., 1st Cadet B. King's R.R.,
Bailey, F. H., 3rd Mx. V. Ar. [L.-Corp.
Bailey, J., jun., H.A.C.
Bailey, J. T., 24th Middlesex R.V.
Baker, C. J., 2nd V.B. Essex Regiment
Baker, F. N., 24th Middlesex R.V.
Baker, H., 4th V.B. Essex Regiment
Baker, H. W., 2nd V.B. R. W. S. Regt.
Baker, W., H.A.C.
Balfour, M., 14th Middlesex R.V.
Ball, S. C., 20th Middlesex R.V.
Ballard, W. G., 1st Middlesex R.V.
Banks, F. L., 1st City of London Rifles
Bannock, W. H., 2nd V.B. Essex
Baragwanath, F., 1st London R. Eng.
Baragwanath, T. P., 1st London R. Eng.
Barden, F. H., 4th V. B. W. Surrey Rgt.
Barnard, J., 21st Middlesex R.V.
Barnard, L. W., 20th Middlesex R.V.
Barnes, A. G., 2nd V.B. E. Sy. Rgt.
Barnett-Smith, G. R., H.A.C., Sergt.
Barnett, H. J., 22nd Middlesex R.V.

---

[1] For Draft, see p. 250. [2] *Westminster Abbey.* [3] *St. Leonard's, Streatham.*
[4] *Westminster Abbey.*

APPENDIX 235

Barnham, L., 3rd Mx. Vol. Artillery
Barrett, A., 2nd City of Ln. Rifles
Barrett, J., 13th Middlesex R.V.
Barrett, J., 1st Cadet Batt. K.'s R.R.
Barrett, F., Per Staff 18th Middlex. R.V., Col.-Sergt.
Barrett, T. B., 7th Middsx. R.V., Sergt.
Barrett, T. C., 19th Middlesex R.V.
Bartlett, C. A., 3rd V.B. East Surrey Reg.
Bartlett, S., 1st Middlesex R.V.
Barton, G. C., 1st City of London Rifles
Bate, F., 1st City of London Rifles
Bates, C. V. de V., H.A.C.
Bates, J. T. G., H.A.C.
Bates, G. W., 18th Middlesex R.V.
Bawden, H. J., 3rd V.B. R. Fusiliers
Baxter, A. E., Worc. Regt.
Bayley, T. D., 1st V.B. Middlesex Reg.
Baynes, C. L., 19th Mx. R.V., L.-Corp.
Beardwell, E. L., 3rd Midx. V. Art., $d.$[1]
Bearman, H. E., 3rd V.B. W. Surrey R.
Beauchamp, A. W., 2nd V.B. Mx. Regt.
Beddow, C. J., 13th Middlesex R. V.
Beeton, T. G., 1st C. of L. R., Col.-Serg.
Beirne, L. G., 21st Middlx. R.V., Corp.
Belcher, E., 1st Surrey Rifles
Belcher, T. P., 21st Middlesex R.V.
Bell, T. J., 5th Middlesex R.V.
Bellairs, C. S., 14th Middlesex R.V.
Belmont, D., 13th Middlesex R.V.
Bence, E. G., 1st V.B. Middlesex Regt.
Bennettt J. F., 4th V.B. W. Surrey Regt.
Bennett, W., 3rd V.B. Royal Fusiliers
Bentley, W. T., 5th Middlesex R.V.
Benwell, E. G., 1st Middlesex R.V.
Best, F., 3rd V.B. E. Surrey Regiment
Best, P. A., 2nd V.B. Mx. R., L.-Corp.
Betterley, C. E. R., H.A.C.
Bettesworth, E., 2nd V.B. W. Surrey R.
Betts, B. B., 1st Lond. Ryl. Eng., Sergt.
Bewsey, A. E., 2nd City of London Rifl.
Beynon, T. J., 1st London Artillery
Biddell, A., 1st Essex Vol. Artillery
Biddell, R. E. W., 15th Middlesex R.V.
Bidgood, G., 2nd (South) Midx. R.V.
Biggin, J. H., 21st Middlesex R.V.
Biggs, F., 2nd V.B. E. Surrey Regt.
Biller, C. W., 2nd City of London Rifles
Billings, W. H., 2nd V.B. E. Surrey R.
Billows, C. D., West Middlesex R.V.
Birch, W. T., West Midx. R.V., Sergt.
Bishop, W. L., 1st Surrey Rifles
Bissett, A., 1st V.B. W. Surrey Regt.
Blaber, W. E., 2nd C. of L. R., L.-Corp.
Black, W., 21st Middlesex R.V.
Blacklin, H., H.A.C.
Blake, W. H., 2nd V.B. W. Surrey R.
Blatt, J., 1st Tower Hamlets R.V., Serg.
Blick, H. A., 4th V.B. E. Surrey Regt.
Blott, J. R., 1st London Royal Eng., $d.$[2]
Blumfeld, S., 1st Midsx. R.V., L.-Sergt.
Blyth, S., 2nd V.B. Essex Rt., L.-Corp.
Blyth, V. T., 2nd Middlesex Vol. Artil.
Boddy, H. F. E., 19th Middlesex R.V.
Bodger, H. L., 13th Middlesex R.V.
Bodger, W. A., 1st Essex V.A., L.-Corp.
Boland, E., 21st Middlesex R.V.
Bolch, H. S., 18th Middlesex R.V.
Bolton, R., 4th V.B. Essex Regiment
Bolton, T., 1st Middlesex Royal Engin.
Bond, H. S., 20th Middlesex R.V.
Bone, H. J., 2nd V.B. Mx. R., Serg., $d.$[3]
Bonner, G. E., 2nd V.B. Essex Regt.
Bonnet, S., 1st London Art., L.-Corp.
Boon, E., 2nd (South) Middlesex R.V.
Boot, C. O., 12th Middlesex R.V.
Booth, A. E., 3rd City of Lon. Rifles
Boswall, J. D., Queen's Royal Scots
Bott, A. E., 3rd V.B. Royal Fusiliers
Boustead, T., 3rd City of Lon. Rifles
Bowden, H. I., 3rd V.B. Royal Fusrs.
Bowles, A. E., 2nd V.B. Middx. Regt.
Bowles, E. G., 3rd V.B. Essex Rgt.
Bowly, E. S. G., 1st Surrey Rifles.
Bowling, T., 3rd V.B. W. Sur. R.,L.-Cp.
Bowman, F., 13th Middlesex R.V.
Boyes, E., 3rd V. B. Royal Fusiliers
Bradley, S. G. L., 13th Mx. R.V., Col-S.
Brady, G. C., H.A.C.
Bragg, A. R., 2nd V.B. Essex Regt.
Braun, C. E. W., 1st V.B. Mx. R., Corp.
Brett, T. P., 12th Middlesex R.V.
Brice, J. H., 13th Middlesex R.V., $d.$[4]
Briggs, A. E., H.A.C.
Briggs, S. W., 12th Middlesex R.V.
Britton, C. A., 1st City of Lon. Rifles
Broadbent, C., 26th Middlesex R.V.
Brockleback, S. H., 13th Middx. R.V.
Brodie, D. G., 19th Midlx. R.V., Corp.
Brook, W. B., 7th Middlesex R.V.
Broome, G., 14th Middlesex R.V.
Brown, A. J., 3rd V.B. E. Surrey Regt.
Brown, A. J. M., H.A.C.
Brown, A. R., 21st Middlesex R.V.
Brown, C. E., 13th Middlesex R.V.
Brown, C. E., 3rd V.B. E. Surrey Rgt.

[1] *Chapel Royal, Savoy.* [2] *St. Barnabas, Wellingborough, North Hants.*
[3] *St. Mary, Staines.* [4] *Not settled.*

APPENDIX

Brown, F., 3rd V.B. E. Surrey Rgt.
Brown, G. J. H., H.A.C.
Brown, H. P., West Mx. Rgt., L.-Corp.
Brown, L. F., 19th Middlesex R.V.
Brown, S. S., 15th Mx. R.V., L.-Sergt.
Brown, T. E., 4th V.B. E. Surrey Rgt.
Brown T. M., H.A.C.
Browning, C., 3rd Middx. Vol. Artilly.
Bruce, M., 19th Middlesex R.V., $d.^1$
Bryant, H. S., 3rd V.B. Royal Fusiliers
Brymer, C. J., H.A.C.
Buckingham, W. H., 1st Ex. V.A., Serg.
Buckland, H. R., 3rd Middx. Vol. Art.
Buckland, R. H., 12th Middlesex R.V.
Buckle, H. O., 14th Midx. R.V., Sergt.
Buckle, H. W., 4th V.B. E. Sur. R., Cpl.
Budd, H. G., 7th Middlesex R.V.
Budd, P. J., 7th Middlesex R.V.
Budd, W. J. C., 13th Middlesex R.V.
Buddell, W. H., 4th V.B. W. Surrey Rgt.
Bull, C., 3rd V.B. Essex Regiment
Buller, A. H. T., 20th Middlesex R.V.
Bulley, C. P., 1st City of Lon. Rifles
Burgess, R., H.A.C.
Burn, A. K., 7th Middlesex R.V.
Burnell, F. J., 3rd V.B. E. Surrey Rgt.
Burrage, C. S., 1st Middlesex R.V.
Burrell, E. G., 1st Tower Hamlets R.V.
Burrett, W. F., 3rd V.B. W. Sur. Rgt.
Burrough, J., 1st City of Lon. Rifles
Burton, G., 22nd Middlesex R.V.
Butler, J. F., 3rd City of Lon. R., Sergt.
Butt, G. K., 1st Middlesex R.V.
Butter, G. W., H.A.C.
Byford, H., 2nd V.B. Essex Regiment
Byng, H. R., 20th Middlesex R.V.
Byron, S. H., H.A.C.

CADDELL, T., Queen's Royal Scots, $c.^a$
Calder, G. J., 7th Middlesex R.V.
Callingham, A., 2nd W. Surrey R.V., $d.^2$
Calver, E. T., 17th (North) Midx. R.V.
Cameron, R. D., 13th Midlsx. R.V., $d.^3$
Camp, J., 15th Middlesex R.V.
Campbell, A., Queen's Royal Scots
Cannon, A. W., West Middsx. R.V., $d.^4$
Capps, W. T., 4th V.B. Essex Regt.
Carden, A., 20th Middlesex R.V., $d.^5$
Carden, H., 5th (West) Middx. R.V.

Carr, J., 3rd City of Lon. Rifles
Carr, S., 13th Middlesex R.V., $d.^6$
Carr, P. J., 1st Essex V.A., Sergt., $d.^7$
Carter, F., 2nd City of London Rifles
Carter, G., 4th V.B. Essex Regiment
Carter, S., Grenadier Guards
Carter, W. J. C., 4th V.B. Essex Regt.
Castle-Smith, H., 20th Mx. R.V., Lance-Corp., $c.^b$
Cates, A. J., 24th Middlesex R.V.
Chadwick, R. S., 14th Mx. R.V., Cpl., $c.^c$
Challen, H. G., 20th Middlesex R.V.
Chalmers, J. M., 1st V.B. W. Sur. Rgt.
Chambers, A. B., 1st Mx. R.V., L.-Cpl.
Chambers, E., H.A.C., Bombdr.
Chambers, J. W., H.A.C.
Chambers, S. H., 1st Lon. Ryl. Engrs.
Chambers, T. A., 5th Middlesex R.V.
Champion, E., 3rd City of Lon. Rifles
Chandler, P., 3rd Middx. Vol. Art.
Chaney, C. R., 1st V.B. W. Sur. Rgt.
Chaplin, A. F., 5th Middlesex R.V.
Chapman, C. J., 3rd Kent V.A., Bombr.
Chapman, H. W., 13th Middx. R.V.
Chappell, A. G., 1st V.B. Middx. Rgt.
Charge, J. A. W., 1st C. of Lon. Rifles
Charles, E. G., 2nd V.B. E. Surrey Regt.
Charleton, E., H.A.C.
Charlton, F. R., 17th Middlesex R.V.
Charlton, G. E., 13th Middlesex R.V.
Chart, S., 22nd Middlesex R.V.
Charter, W. H., 21st Middlesex R.V.
Cheer, B., 2nd V.B. Essex Rgt., $d.^8$
Cheshire, G., 5th (W.) Middlesex R.V.
Cheshire, H. R., 22nd Mx. R.V., Sergt.
Cheshire, R., 3rd Middx. Vol. Artillery
Chidgey, L. W., 2nd Kent Vol. Art.
Child, N. G. L., 14th Middlesex R.V.
Childers, R. E., H.A.C.
Chown, F. H., 13th Middlesex R.V.
Chown, R., 4th V.B. W. Surrey Rgt.
Churton, E. D. L., 12th Middx. R.V.
Clapham, C. A., 1st City of Lon. Rifles
Clare, A. S., H.A.C.
Clark, C. H., 3rd Middx. Vol. Art.
Clark, J., Per. St. 5th Md. R.V., Cl.-Serg.
Clarke A. E., 2nd City of Lon. Rifles
Clary, J., 3rd V.B. Essex Regiment
Clatworthy, F. J., 3rd Middx. Vol. Art.
Cleave, A. F., 18th Middlesex R.V., $d.^9$
Clegg, E. S., 14th Middlesex R.V.

---

[1] *Not settled.*   [2] *St. Mark's, Upper Hale, Farnham.*   [3] *Westminster Abbey.*
[4] *St. Stephen's, Portland Town, N.*   [5] *St. Matthew's, Bayswater.*   [6] *Not settled.*
[7] *All Saints', Forest Gate.*   [8] *St. Botolph's, Colchester.*   [9] *St. Pancras Church.*
[a] *K.O.S.B.*   [b] *Lancashire Fusiliers.*   [c] *9th Lancers.*

APPENDIX 237

Clements, A., 21st Middlesex R.V.
Clerke, W. C., 1st Tower Hamlets R.V.
Clifford, H. B., H.A.C., Corp.
Clippingdale, C. H., 1st C. of Lon. R.
Clough, E. M. O., H.A.C.
Cluff, H. W., 20th Middlesex R.V.
Coates, A. J., 1st Essex Vol. Artillery
Cobb, F. G., 5th West Middx. R.V.
Cochrane, F., 3rd Middx. Vol. Art.
Cohen, G. A., H.A.C.
Cohen, L. W., H.A.C.
Cohn, H. O., 1st Middx. R.V.
Cole, A. J., 2nd V.B. W. Surrey, Reg.
Coleman, E. G., 2nd V.B. Middx. Rgt.
Coleman, M. E., 3rd V.B. Royal Fus.
Collard, A. S., 12th Middlesex R.V.
Collins, F. J., 2nd V.B. Middlesex Rgt.
Collum, A. J., 14th Middlesex R.V.
Colmer, G. W., H.A.C.
Commander, H., 3rd C. of Lon. Rifles
Connew, C., 13th Middx. R.V., Sergt.
Coode, E. G., 3rd V.B. W. Surrey Rgt.
Cook, B. R., 3rd V.B. E. Surrey Rgt.
Cook, E. S., 21st Middlesex R.V
Cook, H. H., 2nd City of Lon. Rifles
Cook, R., 3rd City of Lon. Rifles
Cooke, A. F., 3rd Middx. Vol. Art.
Coombe, R. E., 1st C. B. King's R. R.
Coombs, W. F., 20th Middlesex R.V., *d*.[1]
Cooper, A., 3rd V.B. E. Surrey Regt.
Cooper, C. E., 1st V.B. Essex Regt.
Cooper, C. H., 16th Middlesex R.V.
Cooper, G. W., 4th V.B. Essex, *d*.[2]
Cooper, P. C., H.A.C., Corp.
Cooper, T., 1st Tower Hamlets R.V.
Cope, A. F., 15th Middlesex R.V.
Corbould, P. S., 20th Middlesex R.V.
Cordell, G. W., 17th Middlesex R.V.
Cordon, G. R., 3rd V.B. Royal Fus.
Corfield, R., H.A.C.
Corley, T. J., 2nd Tower Hamlets R.V.
Costin, A. H., 2nd City of Lon. Rifles
Cotter, T. W., 1st Tower Hamlets R.V.
Coulton, G., 16th Middlesex R.V.
Coureaux, A., 16th Middlesex R.V.
Cowin, N. T., 20th Middlesex R.V.
Cowtan, W. F., 19th Midx. R.V., Sergt.
Cox, A. B., 16th Middlesex R.V.
Cox, J. G., 4th V.B. Essex Regiment
Crabb, W., 3rd V.B. Ex. Reg., L.-Corp.
Craik, G. L., 14th Middlesex R.V.
Crampton, G. L., 12th Middlesex R.V.
Cranfield, E. G. S., 7th Middlesex R.V.

Crawhall, H. C., 14th Mx. R.V., L. Corp.
Crick, E. C., 12th Middlesex R.V.
Cripps, F. R., 12th Middlesex R.V.
Crombie, A. E., 1st Sur. Rifles, Cl.-Serg.
Crome, C. C., 16th Middlesex R.V.
Crome, H. T., 16th Middlesex R.V.
Crone, J. S., 13th Middlesex R.V.
Croxon, S., 13th Middlesex R.V.
Crozier, J. W., 2nd V.B. Essex Regt.
Crux, A. G., 4th V.B. E. Surrey Regt.
Cunnington, H. W., 3rd V.B. Ryl. Fus.
Curling, A. I., 16th Middlesex R.V.
Currie, F. W. S., 13th Middlesex R.V.
Curry, W. W., 4th V.B. Essex Regt.
Curtis, F., 4th V.B. W. Surrey Regt.
Curtis, H., 1st Tower Hamlets R.V.
Curtis, L., 14th Middlesex R.V.
Cutler, H., 2nd V.B. Midx. Regt., Corp.
Cutting, C., 3rd V.B. E. Surrey Regt.

Dale, J., Scots Guards (servant)
Dale, J. C., H.A.C.
Dalmahoy, P. C., Queen's Royal Scots, *c*.[a]
Daniel, F., 13th Middlesex R.V.
Daniel, J. W., 19th Middlesex R.V.
Daniels, R. W., 1st V.B. Middlesex Rt.
Darville, H. A., 16th Middlesex R.V.
Davern, R. F., 13th Midx. R.V., Corp.
Davey, A. H., 1st V.B. Essex Regt.
Davey, H., 2nd V.B. Essex Regt.
Davey, J., 3rd V.B. Essex Regt.
David, J. N., 3rd Middlesex Vol. Art.
Davidson, J. S., 4th V.B. E. Surrey Rgt.
Davies, C. J., 1st City of London Rifles
Davies, E. J. W., 5th (W.) Midx. R.V.
Davies, W. E., 1st City of London R.
Davis, A. E., 3rd V.B. Essex Regt.
Davis, E. W., 1st V.B. Essex Regt.
Daws, A. F., 2nd V.B. Middlesex Regt.
Dawson, A. H., 1st Middlesex R.V.
Dawson, E. A., 14th Middx. R.V., *d*.[3]
Day, A., 1st Tower Hamlets R.V.
Day, C. J., 1st Tower Hamlets R.V., *d*.[4]
Day, E. C. F., 1st Middlesex R.V., *d*.[5]
Deane, A. G., 1st Sussex V.A.
Dendy, T. J., 3rd V.B. E. Surrey Regt.
Dennison, H., 3rd V.B. E. Surrey Regt.
Devenish, F. W., 3rd V.B. E. Sur. Regt.
De Witt, V., 13th Middlesex R.V.
Dibbs, S. E., 4th V. B. W. Surrey Regt.
Difford, W., 3rd Kent V.A., S.-Wheeler
Dight, W. J., 2nd City of Lond. Rifles
Dillingham, J., 17th (North) Midx. R.V.

---

[1] *Metlingham, Suffolk.*   [2] *St. Mary's, Ashwell, Herts.*   [3] *Tooting Graveney, Surrey.*   [4] *St. Leonard's, Shoreditch.*   [5] *Not settled.*
[a] *Royal Scots.*

APPENDIX

Dingley, G., 4th V.B. Essex Regt.
Dix, E., 18th Middlesex R.V., L.-Corp.
Dixon, W., H.A.C., Sergt.
Dobree, J. A., H.A.C.
Dodsworth, R. S., 2nd V.B. Midx. Rgt.
Dollar, H. W., H.A.C., Bombr.
Donald, A. P., 7th Middlesex R.V.
Doran, A. C., 2nd V.B. Rl. Fus., L.-Corp.
Double, J. W., 13th Middlesex R.V.
Dowling, M., 2nd V.B. Essex Regt.
Downes, E. H. D., 4th V.B. E. Sur. Rgt.
Dowse, W. J., 3rd V. B., Rl. Fus., Sergt.
Dowsett, E. J., 1st Essex Vol. Artillery
Drawbridge, T. A., 13th Midx. R.V.
Driesen, J. F., 21st Midx. R.V., L.-Sergt.
Drummond, A., 7th Middlesex R.V.
Dudley, T. J., 18th Middlesex R.V.
Dudley, T. W., 1st V.B. Midx. Regt.
Duffitt, T. B., 13th Middlesex R.V.
Duguid, E., 7th Middlesex R.V.
Dunbar, G. J., 4th V.B. E. Surrey Rgt.
Dunbar, S., 1st City of London Rifles,
Duncan, C. L., H.A.C. [L.-Sergt.
Duncan, J. L., 7th Middlesex R.V.
Duncombe, G. F. 3rd Midx. Vol. Art.
Dunk, A. W., 2nd Midx. Vol. Art.
Dunlop, J., 4th V.B. E. Surrey Rgt.
Dunsmore, R., 7th Middlesex R.V.
Durrant, W. H. G., 1st Middlesex R.V.
Dyer, E. A., H.A.C.
Dyer, T., 1st Tower Hamlets R.V., $d.^1$
Dyson, J. S., H.A.C., $d.^2$

EAMES, H. M., 20th Middlesex R.V.
Earle, A. W., 7th Middlesex R.V.
Easey, J. F., 2nd V.B. Essex Regiment
Eastman, H., 1st V.B. Middlesex Regt.
Eatley, A. G., 1st Lon. Royal Engrs., $d.^3$
Eaton, G., Late Gren. Guards, L.-Corp.
Edwards, G., 2nd Kent V.A.
Edwards, G. H., 20th Middlesex R.V.
Edwards, H., 2nd City of London Rifles
Edwards, J., 3rd City of London Rifles
Edwards, P. A., 1st London R.V.
Edwin, J. T., 2nd Middlesex Vol. Artil.
Egerton, V. C., 20th Middlesex R.V.
Elam, H. W. T., H.A.C., Corp., $c.^a$
Ellett, R. E., 1st Cadet Batt. K.R.R.
Elliott, F. P., 2nd Kent Vol. Artillery
Elliot, J. A.G., Queen's Royal Scots, $c.^b$
Elson, R., 2nd V.B. East Surrey Regt.
Elwell, H., 20th Middlesex R.V.

Emson, H. F. Q., 19th Middlesex R.V.
English, W. J., 15th Middlesex R.V.
Esland, T. W., 18th Midx. R.V., Sergt.
Evans, A. E., 4th V.B. W. Surrey Regt.
Evans, A. M., 1st C. of Lon. Rifles, Sergt.
Evans, F. E., 5th (West) Middlesex R.V.
Evans, L. R., 22nd Middlesex R.V.
Everall, H. F., 7th Midx. R.V., L.-Corp.
Everard, H. L., 2nd V.B. Essex Rt., Corp.
Everitt, F. H., 3rd V.B. W. Surrey Regt.
Evitt, H. L., 1st City of London Rifles

FAILES, J. H., 2nd City of London Rifl.
Fairholme, H. W., 20th Middlesex R.V.
Faith, A. W., 1st Cadet Batt. K.R.R.
Faith, F. H., 1st Cadet Batt. K.R.R.
Faizey, W., H.A.C.
Farley, A. E., 1st Tower Ham. R.V., Corp.
Farrell, S. A., 2nd (South) Midx. R.V.
Farrington, E., 2nd V.B. W. Surrey R.,
L.-Corp.
Faulkner, P., 1st V.B. Royal Fusiliers
Fearn, W. R., 18th Middlesex R.V.
Fellows, C. B., 3rd V.B. E. Surrey Regt.
Fenn, G., 5th (West) Middlesex R.V.
Fennell, F. G., 22nd Middlesex R.V.
Fenson, W. H., 18th Middlesex R.V.
Fenwick, G., 2nd V.B. E. Sur. Rt., Sergt.
Fernee, H., 1st V.B. Middlesex Regt.
Fernie, W. J., 14th Midx. R.V., L.-Corp.
Field, J. H. R., 1st Middlesex R.V.
Fielding, H. B., 3rd Midx. Vol. Artillery
Fifield, R. H., 4th V.B. E. Surrey Regt.
Findlay, E. J., 7th Middlesex R.V., Corp.
Firth, A. J., 12th Midx. R.V., L.-Corp.
Fisher, A. G., 1st Middlesex R.V.
Fisher, C. H., 19th Middlesex R.V.
Fisher, G. E., 5th West Middlesex R.V.
Fisher, H. W., 12th Midx. R.V., L.-Corp.
Fisher, T., 5th (West) Middlesex R.V.
Fisk, S. A. M., 26th Middlesex V.R.C.
Fitzclarence, A. A. C., 14th Midx. R.V. $c.^c$
Fitzpatrick, J., 1st C.B. King's Royal R.
Flannagan, D., 1st London R. Engineers
Flannagan, W. J., H.A.C.
Fletcher, J. D., 1st V.B. Middlesex Rgt.
Flewer, A., 2nd City of London Rifles
Flinn, P. T. B., 3rd V.B. Essex Regt.
Flood-Page, A., 7th Middlesex R.V.
Flower, F. H., 1st Essex Vol. Art., L.-Corp.
Flowerdew, H. H., 1st City of Lond. R.
Foden, W., 26th Middlesex V.R.C.

---

[1] *St. Thomas, Bethnal Green.*   [2] *Not settled.*   [3] *St. Mary Magdalene, Holloway.*
[a] *R.F.A.*   [b] *Royal Scots Fusiliers.*   [c] *Royal Fusiliers.*

APPENDIX 239

Follett, F., 1st V.B. Middlesex Regt.
Forbes, L., 7th Middlesex R.V.
Foster, A. H., 1st City of London Rifles
Foster, C. E., 3rd City of London Rifles
Foster, E. C., 20th Middlesex R.V.
Foster, J., 4th V.B. (West) Surrey Regt.
Foulger, A. S., 18th Middlesex R.V.
Fowler, A. J., 19th Middlesex R.V.
Fowler, John, 5th (West) Middlex. R.V.
Fram, J., 21st Middlesex R.V.
Franklin, P. C., 3rd Middlesex Vol. Art.
Frapwell, W. C., 4th Midx. R.V., Corp.
Fraser, M., 7th Middlesex R.V.
Freeland, E. C., 2nd (S.) Mx. R.V., L.-C.
Freeland, M. T., 3rd V.B. E. Sur. Regt.
Freeman, H. E., 2nd V.B. Middx. Rgt.
Freeman, H. E., 1st City of Lond. Rifl.
Freeman, P. A., 2nd V.B. Middlex. Rgt.
French, A. G. P., 4th V.B. E. Sur. Rgt., Corp., d.[1]
French, J. G., 13th Middlesex R.V.
Friend, E. W., 4th V.B. West Surrey Regt.
Fry, H., 2nd Kent Volunteer Artillery
Fuller, E., Permt. Staff 21st Midx. R.V., Col.-Sergt.
Fyson, J. P. P., 26th Middlesex V.R.C.

GALLIFENT, T. M., 2nd V.B. Essex Rt.
Gallon, J., 3rd V.B. Royal Fusiliers
Gamble, G. A. W. F., 1st London R.E., L.-Corp.
Gamble, O. H. C. F., 1st London R.E.
Garbutt, A. W., 1st City of Lond. Artil.
Gardham, Jas., 4th V.B. W. Surrey Regt.
Gardiner, H. E., 1st V.B. Essex Regt.
Garrard, P., 4th V.B. West Surrey Regt., Sergt.
Garrett, H., 3rd City of Lon. Rfl., Corp.
Gascoigne, C. C. H. O., 14th Midx. R.V. c.[a]
Gaskill, G., 13th Middlesex R.V.
Gate, W. P., 1st City of London Rifles
Gatland, W., 1st V.B. Royal Fusiliers
Gazzard, W. R., 22nd Middx. R.V., d.[2]
Geddes, C. W., H.A.C.
Gedge, F. G. P., 13th Middlesex R.V.
Genders, P. R., 13th Middlesex R.V.
German, W. A., 2nd V.B. W. Surrey R.
Gibbons, E. J., 14th Mx. R.V., C.-Sg., d.[3]
Gibbs, W. J., 3rd V.B. Royal Fusiliers
Giles, F. H., 19th Middlesex R.V.
Giles, J. W., 3rd V.B. E. Surrey Regt.
Gill, W. A., 2nd V.B. Middlesex Regt.

Gillard, R. H., 26th Middlesex V.R.C.
Gilliland, W. E., 1st City of London Rif.
Gimsons, S. G., 1st V.B. Middlesex Rgt.
Ginger, A. S., 7th Middlesex R.V.
Glanvill, C. E., 16th Middlesex R.V.
Glassey, P., 1st Tower Hamlets R.V., d.[4]
Glenny, T. A., 7th Middlesex R.V.
Glover, J. A., 7th Middlesex R.V.
Glover, R. H., H.A.C.
Glynn, E. F., 14th Middlesex R.V.
Godard, A. 2nd (South) Middlesex R.V.
Goddard, E., 1st City of Lon. R., L.-Ser.
Goddard, R. B., 21st Middlesex R.V. — I HAVE THIS MEDAL
Godfrey, C. E., 4th V.B. W. Surrey Rgt.
Godley, W., Per. Staff 2nd V.B. R. Fus., Col.-Sergt.
Godwin, G., 2nd V.B. W. Sy. Rgt., Serg.
Godwin, P., 21st Middlesex R.V.
Godwin, R. W. G., 1st City of Lon. Rifl.
Goldsmith, F. H., 13th Middlesex R.V.
Goodall, T. B., H.A.C., Bombr.
Gooding, H., 1st Surrey Rifles
Goodman, T. G., 1st Essex Vol. Artil.
Goodwin, R. W., Late Royal Artillery, Sergt.-Collar-maker
Gossett, F., 16th Middlesex R.V.
Gough, A. W., 12th Middlesex R.V.
Gray, A. J., 22nd Middlesex R.V.
Green, A. E., 2nd V.B. W. Surrey Rgt.
Green, C., 1st V.B. Essex Regt.
Green, D. A., 1st City of London Artil.
Green, J., 2nd V.B. Middlesex Regt.
Green, J. J. R., 4th V.B. Essex Regt.
Greenaway, G., 3rd City of London Rifl.
Greenwell, C. O., H.A.C., c.[b]
Greenwood, C. F. H., 20th Mx. R.V., Ser. Lt. Col.
Greenwood, H., 1st Cadet Batt. K.R.R. 9th, K.O.Y.L
Gregson, A. E., 2nd V.B. Middlesex R. V.C., O.B.E
Greig, L. G., 7th Middx. R.V., L.-Sergt. D.S.O., M.C
Gridley, W. O., H.A.C., Corp.
Griffin, H. W., 19th Middlesex R.V.
Griffiths, T., 5th (West) Middlesex R.V.
Grimsdale, G. C., 12th Middlesex R.V.
Groom, P. J., 20th Middlesex R.V.
Grundy, A. E., Per. Staff 3rd V.B.R. Fu., Col.-Sergt.
Guest, H., 2nd City of London Rifles
Gulson, H., 5th (West) Middlesex R.V.
Gunningham, E., 22nd Mx. R.V., L.-Cp.
Guthrie, G. A., 5th (West) Middx. R.V.
Gutman, W. H., H.A.C., Bombr.
Gutridge, G. W., H.A.C., Bombr.

[1] *Congregational Church, Newport-Pagnell.* [2] *St. Giles-in-the-Fields.* [3] *Hartlebury, Kidderminster.* [4] *Lower Edmonton.*
[a] *Seaforth Highlanders.* [b] *In C.I.V.*

APPENDIX

Haag, O. L., 2nd City of London Rifles
Haddock, A. E., 13th Middlesex R.V.
Hadley, E. H., 2nd (South) Midx. R.V.
Haggard, M., 14th Middlesex R.V.*c*.[a]
Halford, E. S., H.A.C.
Halford, G. E., 1st Middlesex R.V., *d*.[1]
Halford, J. M., 1st Middlesex R. V.
Hall, C., 22nd Middlesex R. V. [Sergt.
Hall, G. W., 1st V.B. Middlesex Regt.,
Hall, H., 3rd Middlesex Vol. Artillery
Hall, J. J., 1st Tower Hamlets R.V.
Hall, W. J. R., 20th Middlesex R.V.
Halls, C., 1st Tower Hamlets R.V.
Hamilton, A. B. B., Queen's Ryl. Scots
Hamilton, W. G., 1st City of Lon. Rifles
Hamilton, N., 1st V.B. Middlesex Rgt.
Hammond, C., 5th (West) Midx. R.V.
Hammond, J., Late R.H.A., Far.-Serg.
Hammond, J. W., 22nd Middlesex R.V.
Hammond, T. E., 2nd City of Lon. Rif.
Hampton, E. B., 1st City of Lon. Rifles
Hampton, J. L., 1st City of Lon. Rifles
Hanckel, A. W., 20th Middlesex R.V.
Hanham, C. R., 1st Tow. Hamlets R.V.
Hanks, A., 1st City of London Artillery
Hanlon, M., 2nd City of London Rifles
Harden, G., 5th (West) Middlesex R.V.
Harden, H. W., 4th V.B. Essex Regt.
Harding, H. P. E., 1st City of Lon. Rif.,
  L.-Sergt.
Harding, T., 2nd Kent Volun. Artillery
Hards, E. H., 2nd V.B. E. Sy. Rgt., Crp.
Hards, T., 5th (West) Midx. R.V., Corp.
Hardy, G., 1st Tower Hamlets R.V.
Harley-Mason, A. E., 13th Middx. R.V.
Harper, A. G. M. N., 12th Middx. R.V.
Harpin, W. S., 1st V.B. Essex Regt.
Harradine, W. J., 3rd V.B. W. Sur. Rgt.
Harris, A. E., 12th Middlesex R.V.
Harris, A. T., 5th (West) Middx. Regt.
Harris, J.W., 4th V.B. West Surrey Rgt.
Harrison, W. G., 4th V.B. W. Sur. Rgt.
Harsum, H. D., 3rd City of Lond. Rifles
Hart, A. E., 2nd (South) Middlesex R.V.
Hart, B. A., 1st City of London Rifles
Hart, N. H., 1st Surrey Rifles, Corp.
Hart, W. B., 12th Middlesex R.V.
Hart, W. P. C., 1st V.B. Middlex. Rgt.
Hartridge, A. E., 21st Middlesex R.V.
Harvey, H., 1st V.B. Essex Regiment
Hasler, H. E., 15th Middlesex R.V.
Hassell, W. H., 1st V.B. Middlex. Rgt.

Hatchard, W., 12th Middlesex R.V.
Hatley, A., 1st Tower Hamlets R.V.
Hatton, W., 15th Middlesex R.V.
Hawes, J. J., 19th Middlesex R.V.
Hawkes, C. W., 20th Middlesex R.V., *d*.[2]
Hawkins, A. K., 1st City of Lon. Rifles
Hawkins, W., 3rd V.B. E. Sy. Rgt., Corp.
Hayes, W. A., 1st Middlesex R.V.
Hayes, W. E., 2nd City of London Rifles
Haylett, R. H., 12th Middlesex R.V.
Haynes, E. E., 13th Middlesex R.V.
Haynes, F. G., 4th Middlesex R.V.
Hazeldine, W. A., 1st Surrey Rifles
Hazell, F. G., H.A.C.
Hector, A., 3rd V.B. East Surrey Regt.
Henderson, D. A., 14th Middlesex R.V.
Henderson, F., 12th Middlesex R.V.
Henderson, G., 17th Middlesex R.V.
Henley, J. H. C., 13th Middlesex R.V.
Henneman, E. G., 1st Cadet Bat. K.R.R.
Henshaw, S. T. W., 1st City of Lon. Rifl.,
  L.-Corp.
Henson, J., 3rd City of London Rifles
Hepburn, F. C., H.A.C.
Herbert, A. F., H.A.C.
Herbert, G., 4th V.B. East Surrey Regt.
Herbert, J. J., 4th V.B. W. Surrey Rgt.
Herbert, W. S., H.A.C.
Hertel, A. C., 16th Middlesex R.V.
Hewitt, W. A. L., 1st V.B. Middx. Rgt.
Hichens, W. L., 14th Middlesex R.V.
Hill, C. P., 13th Middlesex R.V.
Hill, F. A., 3rd Middlesex Vol. Artillery
Hillary, W. M., 21st Middlesex R.V.
Hildred, W. O., 12th Middlesex R.V.
Hills, J. S., H.A.C.
Hills, T., 2nd (South) Middlesex R.V.
Hinton, W., 5th (West) Midx. R.V.
Hitch, P. C., 1st V.B. Essex Regiment
Hoare, G., H.A.C.
Hodgkinson, F., 13th Middlesex R.V.
Hodgkison, H., 5th (West) Middx. R.V.
Holder, G., 4th V.B. Essex Regt., *d*.[3]
Holladay, A. J., 2nd City of Lon. Rifles,
  L.-Sergt.
Holland, C. P., 1st Essex Vol. Artillery
Holland, M. W., 1st City of Lon. Rifles, *d*.[4]
Hollis, G. W., 1st V.B. Middlesex Regt.
Holmes, G. E., 3rd V.B. Roy. Fusiliers
Holmes, W., 1st V.B. Middlesex Regt.
Holt, A. M., 2nd V.B. E. Sy. R., Sergt.
Holt, W. B. L., H.A.C.

---

[1] *Portuguese Synagogue, Lauderdale Road, Maida Vale.*   [2] *St. James's, Piccadilly.*   [3] *Not settled.*   [4] *St. Michael's, Highgate.*
[a] *Welsh Regiment.*

APPENDIX 241

Hooke, J. C., 1st City of London Rifles
Hooper, H. M., H.A.C.
Hopkins, A. H., 1st Mx. R.V., L.-Corp.
Hopkins, E. L., 14th Middlesex R.V.
Hopkins, E. W., 19th Middlesex R.V.
Hopkins, F. M., 2nd V.B. Middl'x Regt.
Horsford, S. G. R., 5th (W.) Midx. R.V.
Houghton, J., 3rd City of Lond. Rifles
Houghton, W. E., 1st City of Lon. R's.
Howes, J., 18th Middlesex R.V.
Hubbard, G. J. S., 3rd Middx. Vol. Art.
Hucker, F. G., 1st Middx. Rl. Engrs., d.[1]
Hudson, C. E., 1st V.B. Middx. Regt.
Hudson, G. M., 4th V.B. Essex Regt.
Huebner, F., 20th Middlesex R.V.
Huggett, G., 2nd Kent Vol. Artillery
Huggins, L. R., 20th Mx. R.V., L.-Corp.
Humphery, T. G. P., 14th Mx. R.V., d.[2]
Humphries, A. J., 17th Middlesex R.V.
Humphreys, J. E., H.A.C.
Hunt, C. W., 3rd V.B. E. Surrey Regt.
Hunt, H., 2nd V.B. Middlex. Regt., d.[3]
Hunt, S. V., H.A.C.
Hunter, S. M., 7th Middlesex R.V.
Huntingdon, C. W., 1st Lon. Ryl. Ens.
Hurst, W. R., 16th Mx. R.V., L.-Sergt.
Hutchins, C. A., 4th V.B. W. Surrey Rt.
Hutchins, W., 1st Cadet Batt. K.R.R.
Hutchings, R. S., H.A.C., d.[4]
Hutchinson, R. J., H.A.C.
Hyman, E. R., 1st City of Lon. Rifles

IVES, G. E., 3rd V.B. E. Surrey Regt. d.[5]

JACKSON, C., Grenadier Guards
Jackson, G. E., Queen's Royal Scots
Jackson, G. R., H.A.C.
Jacobs, H. E., 1st V.B. Midx. Regt., Cpl.
Jacobs, I., 3rd V.B. Royal Fusiliers
Jacobs, J., 19th Middlesex R.V.
James, B., 3rd V.B. Essex Regt., d.[6]
James, C., 13th Middlesex R.V.
James, G., 19th Middlesex R.V.
Jamieson, R., 3rd City of Lond. Rifles
Jamieson, W., 20th Middlesex R.V.
Jarrett, C., 2nd (South) Middlesex R.V.
Jarvis, H., 1st V.B. Middlesex Regt.
Jay, A., 2nd V.B. W. Surrey Regt.
Jenkins, J. A., 2nd V.B. W. Surrey Regt.
Jenkinson, L. G., 1st London R. E.
Jenner, G. T., 21st Middlesex R.V.

Jennings, F. A., 5th (W.) Middl'x R.V.
Johnson, A. E., 4th V.B. W. Surrey Rgt.
Johnson, C. F., 15th Middlesex R.V.
Johnson, H. W., 19th Middlesex R.V.
Johnson, T. H. F., 14th Middlesex R.V.
Johnson, T. I., 2nd Middx. Vol. Art.
Johnston, C., 2nd V.B. Royal Fusileers
Johnston, W. G., 2nd V.B. Royal Fus.
Johnston, W., 7th Midx. R.V., Sergt.
Joliffe, N. A., 3rd V.B. E. Surrey Regt.
Jones, A. R., 2nd Middlesex Vol. Art.
Jones, D. B., 3rd V.B. Royal W. Surrey, Corpl., d.[7]
Jones, H. W., 2nd V.B. Royal Fusiliers
Jones, J., 21st Middlesex R.V.
Jones, T., 20th Middlesex R.V.
Jones, T., Per. Staff 2nd V.B. E. Surrey, Col.-Sergt.
Jones, T. A., 13th Middlesex R.V.
Jones, W. G., 26th Midx. V.R.C., L.-Cpl.
Jordan, E. J., 1st Tower Hamlets R.V.
Joseph, A. S., H.A.C.
Joslin, H. E., 1st V.B. Essex Regt.
Judge, F., 1st Midx. R.V., Col.-Sergt.
Julyan, W. E. R., Late Duke of Cornwall's L.I.R.V.
Jury, T. E., 4th V.B. W. Surrey Regt.

KAYE, A. T., 1st V.B. Middlesex Regt.
Keell, S. A., H.A.C.
Kelley, J., 3rd V.B. Essex Regt.
Kemp, A. R., 3rd Midx. Vol. Art., Sergt.
Kendal, J. C., H.A.C., Bombr.
Kendall, F., 1st V.B. Middlesex Regt.
Kennedy, F., 2nd City of Lond. R., L.-C.
Kennedy, H. W., 4th V.B. W. Surrey Regt.
Kenway, H. C., 20th Middlesex R.V.
Kerr, G. W., 20th Middlesex R.V.
Kettley, G., 1st City of London Rifles
Key, D. S., 13th Middlesex R.V.
Kidner, P. C., 20th Middlesex R.V.
Kiernan, T., 2nd City of London Rifles
Kilpin, W. E., 19th Middlesex R.V.
King, C. J., 3rd V.B. W. Surrey Regt. L.-Corpl.
King, G. W., 3rd V.B. Essex Regt.
King, S., 13th Middlesex R.V., Corpl.
Kingsford, D. P., 1st City of Lond. R., Sergt., d.[8]
Kirby, R. H., 1st Essex Vol. Artillery

---

[1] *St. Michael's, Willesden.* [2] *All Saints, Upper Weston, Bath.* [3] *St. Paul's, Brentford.* [4] *St. Luke's, Chelsea.* [5] *Parish Church, Chertsey.* [6] *St. Dogmart's, Mynachlogddn, Pembroke.* [7] *St. Matthias, Up. Tulse Hill.* [8] *All Saints', Whetstone, Middlesex.*

Kirkpatrick, G., 3rd City of Lond. R.
Kitchen, J. F., 1st Midx. R.V., Corpl.
Knight, C., 2nd V.B. W. Surrey Regt.
Knight, C. S., 2nd (South) Midx. R.V.
Knight, T. B., 3rd V.B. E. Surrey Regt.
Knight, V. P., 1st V.B. Middx. Regt.
Knight, W. C., 1st City of Lond. Rifles
Knowles, W. A. C., 1st Midx R.V., Cpl.
Knox, J. T., 13th Middlesex R.V.

LAKE, T. W., 13th Middlesex R.V.
Lambard, C., 3rd V.B. Royal Fusiliers
Lambart, Hon. H. E. S., 14th Middlesex R.V.
Lambert, A. T., 21st Middlesex R.V.
Lancaster, F. E., 1st Cadet B. King's R.R.
Lancaster, W. J., 1st City of Lond. Art.
Landsberg, J., H.A.C.
Landsberger, H. K. A., 13th Midx. R.V.
Lane, H. W., 7th Middlesex R.V.
Langridge, H. J., 2nd East Surrey Regt.
Lankshear, H. G., 4th V.B. Essex Regt., Sergt.
Lapwood, G. H., 1st V.B. Essex Regt.
Law, H. S., H.A.C., Bombr.
Lawrence, L. J., 19th Middlesex R.V.
Lawrence, T. H., 5th (West) Midx. R.V.
Lawson, G. A., 1st Lond. R. Engineers
Lawton, L. E., 19th Middlesex R.V.
Lazell, H. J., 1st V.B. Essex Regiment
Lazell, H. W., 17th (North) Midx. R.V.
Lea, G. W., 1st City of London Art.
Leacock, H. W., 1st City of Lond. Art.
Lebish, A. A., 4th V.B. E. Surrey Regt.
Le Dieu, G. E., 18th Middlesex R.V.
Le Dieu, H. L., 18th Middlesex R.V.
Lee, A., 2nd City of London Rifles
Lee, G. B., 2nd City of London Rifles
Lee, J. S., 20th Middlesex R.V.
Lefroy, T. E., 20th Middlesex R.V.
Lemmens, G. J., H.A.C.
Lemon, F. J., 3rd V.B. East Surrey Regt.
Levermore, A. R., 3rd V.B. East Surrey Regt.
Lewis, A. E., late Rhodesia M. Police
Lewis, A. J., 4th V.B. E. Surrey Regt.
Lewis, C., 3rd Middx. Volunteer Art.
Lewis, D. M., H.A.C.
Lewis, G. M., 21st Midx. R.V., L.-Cpl.
Lewis, H. H., 1st Middlesex R.V.
Lewis, R. P., 14th Middlesex R.V., c.[a]

Lindsell, A., 1st Tower Hamlets R.V.
Lindsey, C. W., 1st City of Lond. Art.
Linsell, N. D., 1st V.B. Essex Regt.
Linsell, W. C., 1st V.B. Essex Regt.
Lipsham, G. W., 1st Middlesex V.R.C.
Lister, J. W., 15th Middlesex R.V.
Lister, H. R., 14th Middlesex R.V.
Little, S. H., H.A.C., L.-Corpl., c.[b]
Littlejohn, E. A., 4th V.B. West Surrey Regt.
Littlejohns, H., 22nd Middlesex R.V.
Lloyd, A. W., 17th Middlesex R.V.
Lloyd, E. H., 1st City of Lond. Rifles
Lloyd, D. E., 24th Midx. R.V., L.-Sergt.
Lloyd, H., 22nd Middlesex R.V.
Lloyd, J. B., 14th Middx. R.V., L.-Cpl.
Lobb, G. S. J., H.A.C., L.-Corp.
Loder, A. S., H.A.C., Sergt.
Loe, H., 2nd V.B., Middlesex Regt.
London, S., 4th V.B. East Surrey Regt.
Long, E. J., 1st City of London Rifles
Long, F. J., 13th Middlesex R.V.
Long, F. W., 1st City of London Art.
Longman, W. R., 21st Middlesex R.V.
Lorimer, G., H.A.C., Bombr.
Low, F. S., 2nd Middx. Vol. Artillery
Lucas, G. J., 18th Middx R.V., Corpl.
Lucas, J. W., 3rd V.B. E. Surrey Regt.
Lucas, F. P., H.A.C.
Luck, F. C., 18th Middx. R.V., Corpl.
Lufflum, T. W., 2nd V.B. Midx. Regt.
Lufkins, H., 1st Middlesex R.V.
Lukey, H., 13th Middlesex R.V.
Lygo, F. C., 3rd V.B. Essex Regiment
Lynch, C., 3rd V.B. Royal Fusiliers

MACDONALD, J., 7th Middlesex R.V., L.-Sergt.
Mackay, A. F., Queen's Royal Scots
Mackenzie, D. M., 12th Middlesex R.V.
Mackey, W. J., 2nd Kent Vol. Art.
Macklin, C. W., 3rd V.B. East Surrey Regt.
Mackney, H., 1st Sussex Vol. Artillery
Maclaine, G., 3rd Middlesex Vol. Art.
Mager, G. E., H.A.C.
Maidment, G., 1st City of London Art.
Maitland, C.A.S., Queen's Royal Scots, c.[c]
Major, L. B., H.A.C.
Male, J. M., 2nd Tower Hamlets R.V.
Mannall, S. G., 1st Essex Vol. Art., Cpl.
Mansbridge, C., 7th Middlesex R.V.
March, J., 1st V.B. Essex Regiment

---

[a] *Devon Regiment.*   [b] *Connaught Rangers.*   [c] *Gordon Highlanders.*

APPENDIX

Marden, G. W., 1st V.B. Essex Regt.
Margetson, L., 20th Middlesex R.V.
Marin, A. E. A., 21st Middlesex R.V.
Marks, H., 3rd Middlesex Vol. Art., d.[1]
Marsh, L. A., 13th Middlesex R.V.
Marsh, S. W., 1st Middx. R.V., Sergt.
Marshall, C. B., 14th Middlesex R.V.
Martin, A. J., 13th Middlesex R.V.
Martin, D., 1st Sussex Vol. Artillery
Martin, F., 19th Middx. R.V., L.-Corpl.
Martin, F. T., 3rd V.B. E. Surrey Regt.
Martinson, R. L., 4th V.B. E. Sur. Regt.
Mason, A. G., 21st Middlesex R.V.
Masters, G. L., 2nd V.B. Essex Regt.
Mate, C. J., H.A.C.
Mathison, J., 4th Middx. R.V., L.-Sergt.
Matthews, H. W., 3rd V.B. Essex Regt.
Mayes, C. T., 2nd (South) Middx. R.V.
Mayhew, C. H., 18th Middlesex R.V.
McBride, G., 1st V.B. W. Surrey Regt.
McCulloch, A. J., 14th Middx R.V., c.[a]
McCulloch, W., 18th Middlesex R.V.
McDonald, H., 2nd Kent Vol. Artillery
McDonell, F., 7th Middlesex R.V.
McDonell, G. L., 7th Middlesex R.V., Col.-Sergt.
McDougall, H., H.A.C.
McDowell, H., 1st City of London Art.
McFadden, J., Depot R.A. (servant)
McIlraith, E. R., 1st Surrey Rifles
McKewan, A. E., 1st Tower Hamlets R.V.
McLean, T. N., 7th Middlesex R.V.
McNeil, L. J., 30th Co. S.D.R.V. (servt.)
Mears, H. H., 12th Middlesex R.V.
Mellers, R. A., 16th Middlesex R.V.
Mellish, A. D., 12th Middlesex R.V.
Mellor, G., 14th Middlesex R.V.
Mellor, T. K., 3rd V.B. E. Surrey Regt.
Melville, W. W., 14th Middlesex R.V.
Mentz, S. V., 3rd V.B. Royal Fusiliers
Meredith, H. C. W., 1st Middlesex R.V.
Merritt, E., 3rd City of London Rifles
Messenger, C. W., 22nd Middlesex R.V.
Messom, H., 20th Middlesex R.V.
Michael, L. A. C., 1st City of Lond. Art.
Middleton, F., 2nd V.B. W. Sur. Regt.
Middleton, J. C., 15th Middlesex R.V.
Midy, L., 1st V.B. Royal Fusiliers
Millard, E. G., 3rd V.B. E. Surrey Regt.
Miller, G. H., 19th Middlesex R.V.
Miller, H. A., 2nd V.B. Essex Regt., d.[2]
Miller, J. A., 1st City of London Rifles

Millett, H. H., 1st Middx. R.V., L.-Sgt.
Millidge, H. A., 15th Middlesex R.V.
Millidge, H. W., 15th Middlesex R.V.
Mills, W., 1st V.B. West Surrey Regt.
Milne, H. F., 1st V.B. W. Surrey Regt.
Milne. J., Queen's Royal Scots
Milne, M. B., H.A.C,
Milroy, E. A. W., 14th Midx. R.V.
Mitchell, A. R., 3rd Midx. Vol. Artil.
Mockford, W. H., 1st London R. Eng.
Moeller, A. H., H.A.C.
Mollett, H. B., 7th Middlesex R.V.
Monk, A. C., 17th (North) Midx. R.V., Sergt.
Montagnani, W. E. M., 17th Mdx. R.V.
Monteith, B. J., Queen's Royal Scots
Moon, C. F., 1st V.B. Midx. Regt.
Moore, C., 3rd Midx. Vol. Artillery
Moore, E., 22nd Middlesex R.V.
Moore, H. P., 2nd City of Lond. Rifles, Sergt.
Moore, H. W., 16th Middx. R.V., L.-Cp.
Moore, J. W., 1st Surrey Rifles
Moore, S., 12th Middlesex R.V.
Moore, S., 3rd Middlesex Vol. Art.
Moran, W. J. D., 1st V.B. Midx. Regt.
Mordin, A. J., H.A.C.
Morford, D. R., H.A.C.
Morgan, C. V., 13th Middlesex R.V.
Morgan, R. H., 1st Middlesex R.V.
Morris, E. G., 2nd V.B. Midx. Regt.
Mortimer, A. J., 2nd Midx. Vol. Artil.
Moss, W., 5th (West) Midx. R.V.
Mosley, J. W. P., 14th Middlesex R.V.
Mourant, R. W., 19th Middlesex R.V.
Mumford, W. B., 7th Middlesex R.V.
Mumford, W. G., H.A.C.
Murdoch, L. M., H.A.C.
Murnane, G. F. T., H.A.C.
Murphy, H. A., 21st Middlesex R.V.
Murray, H. E. S., 7th Middlesex R.V.
Murrell, A. R. T., 21st Middlesex R.V.
Murrell, W. H., 1st Sussex Vol. Artil.
Mustoe, E. F., 2nd City of Lond. Rifles

Nash, A., 21st Middlesex R.V.
Nash, F., 3rd V.B. W. Surrey Regt.
Nash, F., 4th V.B. W. Surrey Regt., Cpl.
Nash, F. H., 13th Middlesex R.V.
Neame, B., 4th Middlesex R.V.
Negus, F. J., 21st Middlesex R.V.
Nelson, F., 21st Middlesex R.V.
Nelson, R. L., H.A.C., Bombr.

---

[1] *Not settled.*   [2] *Wesleyan Chapel, Colchester.*
[a] *Highland L. I.*

APPENDIX

Nepean, L. St. V., 20th Middlesex R.V.
Nesham, C. F., H.A.C., *c.*[a]
Nesham, H. P., 7th Middlesex, R.V.
Neuff, A. E., 19th Middlesex R.V.
Newey, W. H., 18th Middlesex R.V.
Newland, T. G., 2nd City of Lond. R.
Newson, S. C., 1st V. B. Essex Regt.
Newson, W. F. K., 12th Midx. R.V.
Nichols, C. E., 1st City of London R.
Nichols, W., 22nd Middlesex R.V.
Nicol, B. H., 1st Cad. Bat. King's R.R.
Nightingale, E. W., 1st Cadet B. King's R.R., Corpl.
Nixon, C. F., 13th Middlesex R.V., *d.*[1]
North, A., 3rd City of London Rifles
North, H. C., 21st Middlesex R.V.
Northcott, W., 1st V.B. Midx. Regt.
Norton, E. S., 3rd Midx. Vol. Artillery

O'CONNELL, G. J., H.A.C., Sergt.
O'Connor, T., from Per. Staff 14th Middlesex, Col.-Sergt.
Oexle, W. H., 1st City of London R.
O'Halloran, S. N. E., 20th Midx. R.V., L.-Corpl.
Oliver, A. A., 12th Middx. R.V.. Sergt.
Orbell, J., 2nd V.B. Essex Regt.
Orchard, T. A., 1st V.B. W. Surrey Rgt.
O'Regan, J. F., H.A.C.
Orme, H. S., 18th Middlesex R.V.
Ormrod, E. H., 13th Middlesex R.V.
Osborn, F. H., 3rd V.B. Essex Regt.
Osborn, G. W., H.A.C., Corpl.
Osmond, C. F., H.A.C.
Overton, E. A., 2nd V.B. Midx. Regt., L.-Corpl.
Owers, J., 17th Middlesex R.V.
Owlett, C. S., 4th V.B. W. Surrey Regt.
Oxer, W. A., 2nd V.B. Middlesex Regt.
Oxley, W., 3rd City of London Rifles

PADFIELD, F. H., 20th Middlesex R.V.
Page, A. R., H.A.C.
Page, E. J., H.A.C.
Page, H. N., 12th Middlesex R.V.
Page, W. E., 1st London Royal Engrs.
Page, W. W., 2nd (South) Midx. R.V.
Paine, C., 22nd Middlesex R.V.
Palles, W. F., H.A.C.
Palmer, G., 3rd V.B. Royal Fusiliers
Palmer, H. O., 3rd Midx. Vol. Art., *d.*[2]
Palmer, R., H.A.C., Col.-Sergt.
Palmer, W., 4th V.B. East Surrey Regt.

Park, C. N., 21st Middlesex R.V.
Park, W. J., 1st Tower Hamlets R.V., Sergt.
Parker, W. C., 3rd Middlesex Vol. Artl.
Parsley, A. J., 1st Middx. R.V., Sergt.
Parsons, F., 1st Middlesex R.V.
Parsons, G. W., 3rd City of London Rifles
Parsons, H. D., 1st V.B. Midx. Regt.
Parsons, W. J., 20th Middlesex R.V.
Passmore, A., 20th Middlesex R.V.
Patey, A. J., 1st City of Lond. Art., Sgt.
Patten, F., 1st Tower Hamlets, R.V.
Pattenden, P. B., 13th Middlesex R.V.
Paul, A. L., 1st City of London Rifles
Paul, G. H., 1st City of London Rifles, L.-Corpl.
Pausch, J. C., 1st City of London Artil.
Payne, W. H., 1st V.B. W. Surrey Rgt., Corpl., *d.*[3]
Paynter, J., 1st City of London Rifles
Pearce, D. C., 18th Middlesex R.V.
Pearce, F., 3rd City of London Rifles
Pearce, R. R., 3rd V.B. Royal Fusiliers, L.-Corpl.
Pearson, W. S., 2nd V.B. Midx. Regt.
Pegg, G., 2nd Middlesex Vol. Artillery
Pegler, B. C. H., 2nd (S.) Midx. R.V.
Pellett, V. T. N., 2nd Midx. Vol. Artil.
Pemberton, S. A., 1st London R.E.
Penn, H. E., 16th Middlesex R.V.
Pether, C. J., 1st V.B. Essex Regiment
Perkins, H. M., H.A.C.
Perkins, H. W., H.A.C.
Perkins, W. H., 1st V.B. Midx. Regt.
Perry, G. B., 2nd Middlesex Vol. Artil.
Petty, L. G., 1st City of London Rifles
Petterson, L., 17th (North) Midx. R.V.
Phillips, C. E., 1st City of London R.
Phillips, C. J., 2nd V.B. Royal Fus.
Phillips, C. V., 4th V.B. W. Surrey Rgt.
Phillips, E. G., 2nd City of London R.
Phillips, G., 2nd V.B. Essex Reg., Corp.
Phillips, L. J. A., 2nd (South) Mx. R.V., L.-Corpl.
Phipps, T., 5th (West) Middlesex R.V.
Pickman, F. J., 13th Middlesex R.V.
Pigou, H. J., 1st V.B. Royal Fusiliers
Pilgrim, H., 1st Essex Vol. Artillery
Pink, A. D., 13th Middlesex R.V.
Pitcairn, G. E., 12th Midx. R.V., L.-Cpl.
Pitt, P. H., 2nd Middlesex Vol. Artil.
Pitts, C. E., 13th Middlesex R.V.

---

[1] *Not settled.*   [2] *St. Marylebone Parish Church.*   [3] *S. Mark's, South Norwood.*
[a] *C.I.V*

APPENDIX 245

Platt, W. L., 1st V.B. Essex Regt.
Pocock, G. B., 1st City of London R.
Pole, E. H., 2nd City of London R.V.
Pollard, G. E. F., H.A.C.
Pollett, C. A., 22nd Middlesex R.V.
Pollock, D. W., 1st City of London R.
Poole, P., 2nd Tower Hamlets R.V., *d.*[1]
Portch, J. W., H.A.C.
Potter, C. W., 1st City of London R.
Potter, E. A., 2nd V.B. Essex Regt., Cpl.
Powell, S. H., 2nd Middx. V.A., L.-Cpl.
Powter, W., 1st V.B. Essex Regiment
Prendergast, H. W., H.A.C.
Presland, G., 21st Middlesex R.V.
Preuss, A. R. W., 19th Middx R.V., *d.*[2]
Price, D. R., 4th V.B. East Surrey Rgt.
Prince, C. H., 4th V.B. East Surrey Rt.
Prior, A., 3rd V.B. Essex Regiment
Pritchard, A., 3rd Middlesex Vol. Artil.
Prudence, F., 2nd V.B. Midx. Regt.
Pryce, J. C., 19th Middlesex R.V.
Pugh, G. W., 1st Surrey Rifles, Sergt.
Pugsley, E. O., 2nd Middlesex V.A.
Pullen, G., 3rd V.B. East Surrey Rgt.
Punter, J., 2nd V.B. West Surrey Regt., L.-Corp.
Purnell, G. E., 1st Middlesex R.E.
Pursaill, J. T., 3rd Middlesex V.A.
Putland, L. P., 13th Middlesex R.V.
Pye, S. J., 1st Essex Volunteer Artillery
Pyke, T. J., 1st Middlesex R.V.
Pyne, F. J. M., 20th Middlesex R.V.

RADDON, W. M., 1st V.B. Midx. Regt.
Raisbeck, G., 1st Sussex Vol. Artillery
Ramsey, H. B., H.A.C.
Ramsley, F. J., 17th (N.) Middx. R.V., L.-Corp.
Randall, J. C., 24th Middlesex R.V.
Ransome, H. J., 5th (W.) Midx. R.V.
Rantell, A. J., 4th V.B. E. Surrey Regt.
Rantell, W. C., 4th V.B. E. Surrey Rgt.
Rapley, W. W., 3rd V.B. Essex Regt.
Rapson, S. C., 17th (N.) Midx. R.V.
Rawlings, H., 3rd V.B. W. Surrey Rgt.
Rawlings, H. W., 22nd Middlesex R.V.
Raynor, C. S., 13th Middlesex R.V.
Razzell, W. L., 2nd V.B. E. Surrey Rt.
Read, H., 1st V.B. W. Surrey Regt.
Read, J., 5th (W.) Middx. R.V., Sergt.
Reading, C. H. R., 3rd V.B. E. Sur. R.
Reading, J. W., 12th Middlesex R.V.
Redmond, C. J., 19th Middlesex R.V.

Reed, W., 12th Middlesex R.V.
Reid, W., 2nd Kent Vol. Artillery
Reidpath, A., 4th V.B. W. Surrey Rgt.
Renshaw, W. W., 14th Middlesex R.V.
Reynolds, H. L., 4th Middlesex R.V.
Rich, W. A., H.A.C.
Richards, C. J., 4th V. B. E. Surrey R.
Richards, H. P., 1st Surrey Rifles, L.-Cp.
Richards, R. G., 1st Tow. Hamlets R.V.
Richardson, A. F., 13th Middlesex R.V.
Richardson, W., 2nd V.B. Middlesex R.
Rider, J. W., 19th Middlesex R.V.
Ritchie, G. O., H.A.C.
Ritchie, R., 1st V.B. Middlesex Regt.
Robbins, D. G., H.A.C.
Roberts, F., 3rd Middlesex V. Artill.
Roberts, F. C., 2nd Middlesex V.A.
Roberts, G., 17th (N.) Midsx. R.V., *d.*[3]
Roberts, W. D., 1st Tow. Hamlets R.V.
Robertson, H. C., 7th Middlesex R.V.
Robertson, T., 7th Middlesex R.V.
Robinson, E. W., 21st Middlesex R.V.
Robinson, H. L., 20th Middlesex R.V.
Robinson, J. A., 4th V.B. Essex Regt.
Robinson, T. T., 20th Middlesex R.V.
Rodgers, J., 20th Middlesex R.V.
Rogers, T. G., 5th Middlesex R.V.
Romer, A., 19th Middlesex R.V.
Romer, H., 19th Middlesex R.V.
Roos, C. E., 13th Midlx. R.V., L.-Cpl.
Roper, E., 2nd V.B., E. Surrey Regt.
Rosenthal, L., 3rd Middlesex V. A.
Ross, G. W., 3rd V.B. E. Surrey Regt.
Ross, J. A., 12th Middlesex R.V.
Ross, J. E. E., 4th V.B. W. Surrey Rgt.
Rowe, A. E., 3rd V.B. E. Surr. Rgt., *d.*[4]
Rowles, B. H., 3rd Middlesex V. Artill.
Royal, W., 2nd City of London Rifles
Ruddle, C. W., 1st City of London R.
Ruddock, E. H. M., 1st V.B. W. Surrey Regiment
Rusby, E. L. M., H.A.C.
Rushworth, S., 22nd Middlesex R.V.
Rust, P., 20th Middlesex R.V., Sergt.
Ryder, A. H., 3rd Middlesex V. Artill.

SADDLER, H., 21st Middlesex R.V.
Salinger, A., 1st Middlesex R.V.
Samways, R. P., 21st Middlesex R.V.
Sandelands, P. E., 14th Middlesex R.V.
Sanders, G., 1st Middlesex R.E.
Sargent, F. R., 3rd V.B. Rl. Fus., L.-C.
Sargent, G. E., 2nd V.B. W. Sur. R., *d.*[5]

---

[1] *Trinity Chapel, E. India Docks.*   [2] *St. George the Martyr, Queen's Square, W.C.*   [3] *St. Michael's, Camden Town.*   [4] *Chertsey.*   [5] *Horley, Surrey.*

APPENDIX

(margin note: I HAVE THIS MEDAL —)

Sare, T. H., 13th Middlesex R.V.
Saunders, A. T., 1st V.B. Midx. Regt.
Saunders, C. E., 1st V.B. Midx. Regt.
Saunders, F., 2nd V.B. Essex Regt.
Savage, H., 1st Sussex Vol. Artillery
Saville, C. F., 2nd V.B. Essex Regt.
Sawle, W. E., 1st Sussex Vol. Artillery
Sawyer, H. H., H.A.C.
Say, J., 1st Tower Hamlets R.V., d.[1]
Sayer, W., 1st V.B. Essex Regt.
Scantlebury, W. A., H.A.C.
Scarborough, E. P., 4th V.B. W. Surrey Regiment
Scarborough, G. A., 3rd V.B. W. Sur. Regiment, Corp.
Scarfe, J. T., 2nd Middlesex V.Artill.
Scheurer, H. F. W., 21st Midx. R.V.
Schneidau, A. E., 1st Middlesex R.V.
Schultz, W. A., H.A.C.
Scott, G., 14th Middlesex R.V., Corp.
Scott, G. H. G., 14th Mx. R.V., Sergt.
Scott, H., 5th (West) Middlesex R.V.
Scott, J., 2nd Kent Vol. Artillery
Scott, J. A., 2nd V.B. Essex Regiment
Scott, R. J., 4th V.B. W. Surrey Rgt.
Scutt, C. S., 5th (West) Middx. R.V.
Seabrook, W. W., 2nd C. of Lon. Rifles
Seccombe, E. A. J., H.A.C.
Seaton, G. S., 14th Middlesex R.V.
Selfe, H. R., 2nd V.B. Mx. Rgt., Cpl.
Semper, W., 3rd V.B. Royal Fusiliers
Semple, W. A., 1st City of Lon. Rifles
Sendall, A. P., 2nd V.B. Royal Fus.
Seyfang, H., 1st Surrey Rifles
Seymour, W., Per. Staff 4th V.B. W. Surrey, Col.-Sergt.
Shaw, F., 22nd Middlesex R.V.
Shaw, W. H., 3rd V.B. W. Sur. Regt.
Shearman, A. E., H.A.C. [Sergt.
Shears, M. E., 16th Midlx. R.V., Sergt.
Sheath, W. A. S., 2nd (S.) Middx. R.V.
Sheen, C., 1st Tower Hamlets R.V.
Sheffield, J. E., 1st City of London Art.
Shepherd, J. B., 17th Middlesex R.V.
Shepherd, W. E., 2nd C. of Lon. Rifles
Sheppard, F. S., 13th Middlesex R.V.
Sherwood, E. C., 1st Cadet Bat. K.R.R.
Short, A. R., 5th (West) Middx. R.V.
Short, J. A., 1st Middlesex R.V.
Shorter, F. W., H.A.C.
Shorter, R. G., H.A.C.
Shrimpton, W. H., 16th Mx. R.V., d.[2]
Sibbons, F. W., 2nd V.B. Middx. Rgt.

Silly, G. A., 3rd V.B. E. Surrey Rgt.
Silver, W. G., 21st Middlesex R.V.
Simmons, H. G., 1st City of Lon. Art.
Simmons, S. W., 13th Mx. R.V., L.-C.
Sims, A. W., 2nd V.B. W. Surrey R.
Sims, J., 2nd V.B. West Surrey Regt.
Simpson, H. G., 1st City of Lon. R.V.
Sinclair, D., 16th Middlesex R.V.
Singer, W. D., 1st City of Lon. Rifles
Sitwell, W. S., 14th Middlesex R.V.
Skeet, W. G., 1st V.B. Rl. Sussex Regt., Lce.-Cpl.
Skillin, F. J., 1st V.B. Essex Regiment
Skinner, P. R., 3rd V.B. Essex Regt.
Slatter, C. W., 1st City of London Art.
Sleeman, J. L., 21st Middlesex R.V.
Slight, E. W., 2nd City of Lon. Rifles
Slocombe, B. W., 13th Middlesex R.V.
Smart, A., 1st Tower Hamlets R.V.
Smart, F., 13th Middlesex R.V.
Smith, A. C. G., 13th Middlesex R.V., Col.-Sergt.
Smith, C., 22nd Middlesex R.V.
Smith, C., 13th Middlesex R.V.
Smith, E. A., 1st C. of Lon. Ar., L.-Cpl.
Smith, E. J. C., H.A.C.
Smith, F., 1st London Ryl. Eng., Sergt.
Smith, F., 3rd V.B. E. Surrey Regt.
Smith, L., 2nd V.B. Essex Rgt., d.[3]
Smith, P. H., 3rd Middx. Vol. Artillery
Smith, P. T., 3rd V.B. W. Surrey Rgt.
Smith, R., 20th Middlesex R.V.
Smith, R.E., 3rd V.B. Royal Fusiliers
Smith, W., 19th Middlesex R.V.
Smith, W. G., 4th V.B. E. Sur. Regt.
Smith, W. S., 2nd Kent Vol. Artillery
Snelling, E., 2nd V.B. E. Surrey Regt.
Snow, A. W., 2nd City of Lon. Rifles
Snutch, G., 21st Middlesex R.V.
Soffe, F. J., 2nd V.B. Essex Rgt., d.[4]
Soffe, R., 2nd V.B. Essex Regiment
Soller, H. G., 1st London R.E.
Solley, S. W., 1st Surrey Rifles, L.-Cpl.
Somers, J. P., 14th Middlesex R.V.
Somerville, W., 16th Middlesex R.V.
Soons, C. H., 1st V.B. Middx. Regt.
South, H., 1st V.B. Middlesex Regt.
South, T., 2nd Middlesex Vol. Artillery
Southby, E. A. D., 21st Middlesex R.V.
Spicer, T., 1st V.B. Essex Regiment
Spittle, G., 3rd C. of Lond. R., L.-Cpl.
Spon, C. A., 20th Middlesex R.V.
Spratt, H. D., 14th Middlesex R.V.

---

[1] *St. Leonard's, Shoreditch.*   [2] *St. George's, Camberwell.*   [3] *St. Mary's, Chelmsford.*   [4] *All Saints', Maldon, Essex.*

APPENDIX 247

Spurge, C. H., 1st City of Lon. Art.
Stacey, E. C., 2nd Middx. Vol. Art.
Stallard, F. C. F., 14th Mx. R.V., Sergt.
Standen, A. C., H.A.C.
Staples, G., 1st V.B. Middlesex Regt.
Starr, W. J., 3rd V.B. Royal Fusiliers
Stayner, F. J., 1st V.B. W. Surrey Rgt.
Steele, M. C., 1st V.B. Royal Fusiliers
Stenner, A. E., 2nd V.B. Royal Fus.
Stephens, E. J., 1st Essex Vol. Art.
Stephens, H. A. D., 12th Middx. R.V.
Stephenson, R. M., H.A.C.
Sterling, S. E., 24th Middlesex R.V.
Steven, T. E., 3rd Middx. Vol. Art.
Stevens, W. G., 3rd Middx. Vol. Art.
Stewart, E. C., 1st Middlsx. R.V., Cpl.
Stock, F. C., 2nd City of Lon. Rifles
Stockley, H., 2nd V.B. Essex Regt.
Storer, D. D., H.A.C.
Storey, R., 2nd Middx. Vol. Artillery
Strachan, D. J., 2nd City of Lon. Rifles
Stratton, B. E., 3rd Middx. Vol. Art.
Streat, L., 4th V.B. Essex Regiment
Stringer, H. J. T., 1st V.B. Middx. Rgt.
Stromqvist, H. S., 20th Middlesex R.V.
Stroud, A. W. A., 1st T. Hamlets R.V.
Suchwell, L., 1st V.B. Middlesex Regt.
Sugden, G., 13th Middlesex R.V.
Sulivan, P., 2nd V.B. Middlesex Regt.
Sullivan, A., A.S.C. (servant)
Sullivan, J., late 1st Dragoon Guards
Sulman, S. W., H.A.C.
Sumerling, C., 2nd City of Lon. Rifles
Susands, E., 1st Tower Hamlets R.V.
Swift, T. A., 1st Middlesex R.V.
Symes, P. J. T., H.A.C.
Symons, A. F., 2nd T. Hamlets R.V.
Symons, J. G., 2nd (South) Middx. R.V.

TACEY, P. H., H.A.C.
Tanner, A. S., 2nd (South) Middx. R.V.
Tarrant, P. J., 3rd C. of Lon. R., Sergt.
Tasker, E., 18th Middlesex R.V.
Tattershall, F. H., 7th Mx. R.V., $d.$[1]
Taylor, A. E., 21st Middlesex R.V.
Taylor, C. E., 1st C. of Lon. R., L.-Serg.
Taylor, G. S., 3rd V.B. E. Surrey Rgt.
Taylor, H. P. B., H.A.C., L.-Sergt.
Taylor, L., Per. Staff 2nd V.B. Middx., Col.-Sergt.
Taylor, P. S., H.A.C., Sergt.

Tebay, C. H., 3rd Middx. Vol. Art.
Tebbutt, H. C., 12th Middlesex R.V.
Templeman, R. H., 3rd V.B. Essex Regt.
Templar, E. R., 13th Middlesex R.V.
Templing, A. G. A., 3rd V.B. Essex R.
Tetley-Jones, W., H.A.C.
Thatcher, L. S., 2nd V.B. Middx. Rgt.
Thew, G. H., 1st V.B. Middlesex Rgt.
Thick, W. A., 2nd V.B. Middx. R., $d.$[2]
Thin, H. M., 14th Middlesex R.V.
Thomas, F. R., 12th Middlesex R.V.
Thomas, F. W., 3rd V.B. Rl. Fus., Cpl.
Thomas, W. S., 21st Middlesex R.V.
Thompson, E. G., 17th (N.) Midx. R.V.
Thompson, F. G. M., 20th Mx. R.V., $c.$[a]
Thornhill, T., Gren. Guards (servant)
Thorpe, T. W., 2nd V.B. Essex Regt.
Thurlow, A. G., 3rd V.B. Essex Regt.
Thwaite, W., 19th Middlesex R.V.
Timms, F., 2nd West Surrey Regt.
Tipper, V. G., 1st City of Lon. Rifles
Tomkins, C., Per. Staff 17th Mx., Cl.-Sg.
Tomlinson, P., 3rd V.B. E. Surrey Rgt.
Toone, W. G., 1st V.B. Middlesex Rgt.
Towers, F. W., 1st City of London Art., Corp., $d.$[3]
Townshend, B. C., 14th Midsx. R.V., $c.$[b]
Towse, C. H., 20th Middlesex R.V.
Toynbee, T. H., H.A.C.
Tozer, G. T., 19th Middlesex R.V.
Travers, E. W., 1st Tower Ham. R.V.
Tregenza, E. W., 19th Mx. R.V., Corp.
Trew, T. M., 13th Middlesex R.V.
Trew, W. G., 13th Middlesex R.V.
Tricky, F., 5th (West) Middlesex R.V.
Trimmer, G. F., 2nd V.B. W. Sur. Rgt.
Triplett, A. J., 22nd Middlesex R.V
Trussler, T. W., 1st Cadet Batt. K.R.R. — I HAVE THIS MEDAL
Tunbridge, G. C., Per. Staff 3rd V.B. West Surrey, Col.-Sergt.
Tunbridge, G. W. M., 4th V.B. West Surrey Regiment, $d.$[4]
Tuppen, A., 3rd City of Lon. Rifles, $d.$[5]
Turley, W. W., 1st V.B. Royal Fusiliers
Turner, F. N., 20th Middlesex R.V.
Turner, T., 2nd V.B. E. Surrey Regt.
Turner, T. W., 3rd Middx. Vol. Art.
Turrell, J. W., 13th Mx. R.V., Sergt.
Tussler, H. W., 3rd V.B. Royal Fusrs.

---

[1] *St. Paul's, Hammersmith.* [2] *St. Paul's, Brentford.* [3] *Not settled.*
[4] *Camden Church, Camberwell.* [5] *St. John's, Upper Holloway.*
[a] *R.G.A.* [b] *C.I.V.*

APPENDIX

Tyndale, J., 1st Tower Hamlets R.V., *d*.[1]
Tyrwhitt, F. St. J., 13th Middx R.V., *c*.[a]

UNWIN, S. J., H.A.C.

VALENTINE, F. G., 1st Sx. V. Art., Bomb.
Vaughan, C. W. H., 4th V.B. W. Sur. Regiment
Vaughan, I. S., 13th Middlesex R.V.
Vellacott, R. R., 1st City London Art.
Venning, J. R., 1st Middlesex R.V.
Verdon, H., Gren. Grds.
Vernum, A. E. J., 1st V.B. Mx. Rgt., *d*.[2]
Vicary, J. H., 16th Middlesex R.V.
Vickerstaff, E. J., 16th Middlesex R.V.
Vickery, W. C., 18th Middlesex R.V.
Vigor, A. F., H.A.C.
Vigor, F. K., H.A.C.
Vine, G. H. M., H.A.C.
Vine, T. W., 3rd Middx. Vol. Ar., Sergt.
Vivian, E. J., 1st V.B. Royal Fusiliers
Voller, P. F., 17th (North) Middx, R.V.
Waddell, G. F., 2nd (South) Midx. R.V.
Wailes, J. M., 7th Middlesex R.V.
Wakefield, O., 13th Middlesex R.V.
Wakem, T., 2nd V.B. W. Surrey Rgt.
Walford, D. C., 20th Mx. R.V., Corp.
Walker, J. A., 1st City of London Art.
Walker, R. D., 7th Middlesex R.V.
Walker, W., 1st Tower Hamlets R.V.
Walker, W. A., 1st Tow. Ham. R.V., *d*.[3]
Walker, W. O., H.A.C.
Wall, A. E., 16th Middlesex R.V.
Waller, A. E., 1st Middlesex R.V.
Walliss, G., 1st Tower Hamlets R.V., *d*.[4]
Walter, H. G., 2nd Middlesex Vol. Art.
Walter, L., H.A.C., Bombr.
Walter, N., 1st V.B. Essex Regiment
Walters, H. G., 20th Middx. R.V
Walters, T. E., 2nd V.B. Royal Fusrs.
Walls, W., 4th V.B. Essex Regiment
Waltham, R., 1st V.B. Essex Regiment
Walton, E. R., H.A.C.
Walton, J., 2nd V.B. Essex Regiment
Warcup, H. E., 1st C. of Lon. Rfl., Serg.
Ward, F. M., 2nd (South) Middx. R.V.
Ward, H. H., H.A.C., Bombr.
Waring, J. F. (servant)
Warren, C. J., 4th V.B. Essex Regt.
Warren, H. G., 1st Tower Hamlets R.V.
Warren, T., 3rd V.B. Royal Fusiliers

Warren, W. S., 2nd Tr. Hs. R.V., Corp.
Wason, R., 14th Middlesex R.V.
Waterhouse, J., 3rd V.B.W. Sur. Rgt., *d*.[5]
Waters, R. W., 1st City of Lon. Rifles
Watkins, F. J., 3rd V.B. Essex Regt.
Watson, R. J., 2nd Middx. Vol. Art.
Watt, H. A., 21st Middlesex R.V.
Watts, F. T. F., 12th Middlesex R.V.
Webb, C. C. W., 1st C. of Lon. Rifles
Webb, H. G., 1st V.B. Royal Fusiliers
Webb, W., 3rd City of London Rifles
Webber, W. B. I., 14th Middlesex R.V.
Weekes, H. E., 20th Middlesex R.V. *c*.[b]
Weeks, R., 20th Middlesex R.V.
Weller, F., 1st V.B. Royal Fusiliers, L.-C.
Wells, T. W., 1st Tower Hamlets R.V.
Welsh, G. N. M, 13th Middlesex R.V.
Welsh, R. H., 4th V.B. W. Sur. Rgt.
Welsh, R. W. W., 4th V.B. Essex Rgt.
Wenham, R. T., 3rd Middx. Vol. Art.
Wensley, A., 1st London Royal Engnrs.
Wernham, G., 3rd V.B. E. Sur. Regt.
Wesson, W. J., 15th Middlesex R.V.
Westacott, E. G., 1st Middlesex R.V.
Westcott, F., 19th Middlesex R.V.
Weston, C.IJ. G., 2nd V.B. W. Sur. R., *d*.[6]
Weston, M. S., 20th Middlesex R.V.
Westwood, J. W. J., 24th Middx. R.V.
Wheeler, A. C., 1st Middx. Ryl. Engrs.
Wheeler, F. W., 12th Middlesex R.V.
Wheeler, F. W., 26th Middx. R.V.
Whitaker, T., 4th V.B. E. Surrey Rgt.
White, A., 13th Middlesex R.V.
White, E. W., 3rd Middx. Vol. Art.
White, J., 16th Middlesex R.V.
White, J., 13th Middlesex R.V., L.-Corp.
White, W., 1st V.B Essex Regiment
Whitehead, F. C., H.A.C.
Whitehead, F. G., 4th Middlesex R.V.
Whitehead, R. H., H.A.C.
Whitehead, R. H., 13th Middlesex R.V.
Whitelaw, G. A., 1st Middlesex R.V.
Whittome, J. O., H.A.C.
Whyntie, J. J., 1st V.B. Royal Fusiliers
Wickens, A., 4th V.B. Es. Reg., L.-Corp.
Widdows, W. W., 2nd V.B. Midx. Rgt.
Wild, G., 1st Tower Hamlets R.V.
Wild, W., 17th Middlesex R.V.
Wilkes, H. A., 4th V.B. Essex Regt.
Wilkins, G. H., 3rd V.B. Essex Regt.
Wilkins, R., 13th Middlesex R.V.

---

[1] *Not settled.*   [2] *Smallarms Factory Church, Enfield.*   [3] *Not settled.*
[4] *St. Luke's Church, E.C.*   [5] *Not settled.*   [6] *St. Peter's, Godalming.*
[a] *Worcester Regiment.*   [b] *West Indian Regiment.*

APPENDIX 249

Wilkinson, E., 1st V.B. Middlesex Rgt.
Wilkinson, L. C. G., 14th Middx. R.V.
Wilkinson, W., 1st Middlesex R.E.
Wilcocks, A. J., 1st V.B. Middx. Rgt.
Wilcocks, M. F., 1st City of Lond. Rifles
Willett, P. A., 2nd V.B. W. Surrey Rgt.
Williams, A., 2nd Kent Vol. Artillery
Williams, A. F. B., H.A.C.
Williams, B. G., 1st Surrey Rifles
Williams, B. J., 21st Middlesex. R.V., d.[1]
Williams, E. P., 20th Mx. R.V., L.-Corp.
Williams, E. J., 18th Middlesex R.V.
Williams, W. F. H., 1st V.B. Ryl. Fusl.
Williams, G. M., 1st City of Lond. Rifles
Williams, R. M., 2nd V.B. Mx. R., Serg.
Willoughby, P. H., 3rd V.B. W. Sur. R.
Willows, G. W., 7th Mx. R.V., L.-Corp.
Wills, R. H., 21st Middlesex R.V.
Willsher, J. W., 1st Tower Hamlets R.V.
Wiltshire, A., 16th Middlesex R.V.
Wilson, F. J., 1st V.B. Mx. Regt., Corp.
Wilson, G. F., 1st City of London Rifles
Wilson, H. F., 3rd V.B. E. Surrey Rgt.
Wilson, T. W., 3rd City of Lond. Rifles
Wilson, W., 3rd V.B. Essex Regiment
Wilson, W. S., 7th Middx. R.V., Corp.
Wilton, L. E., H.A.C.
Windsor, A. H., 3rd Midx. Vol. Artillery
Wink, A. A., H.A.C., Bombr.
Wisdom, J. A., 21st Middlesex R.V.
Wood, A. E., H.A.C., Sergt.
Wood, A. L., H.A.C.
Wood, C., 1st V.B. Essex Regiment
Wood, G. J., 4th V.B. East Surrey Rgt.

Wood, H., 4th V.B. Essex Regiment
Wood, W. E., 12th Mx. R.V., L.-Corp.
Woodford, W., 13th Middlesex R.V.
Woodman, W., 3rd Mx. Vol. Art., Corp.
Woods, E. A., 18th Middlesex R.V.
Woodward, G. E, 3rd V.B. E. Sur. Rgt.
Woodyard, J. A., 2nd V.B. Essex Regt.
Woolhouse, H., 19th Middlesex R.V.
Wooton, H. D., 2nd (South) Midx. R.V.
Worrall, E. W., 3rd Middlesex Vol. Art.
Worsfold, J. L., 12th Midx. R.V., Corp.
Wright, A. G., 2nd Middlesex Vol. Art.
Wright, C., H.A.C., Bombr.
Wright, E. C., 20th Mx. R.V., L.-Cor.,c.[a]
Wright, H. W., 2nd V.B. W. Surrey Rt.
Wright, J. S., 2nd City of London Rifles
Wright, R. A., 1st London Ryl. Engin.
Wright, S. E., 2nd V.B. Middlesex Rgt.
Wright, W., 2nd V.B. Essex Regiment
Wright, W. C., 1st V.B. Es. R., L.-Corp.
Wright, W. S., Per. Staff 13th Mx., C.-Sr.
Wyatt, A., 3rd City of London Rifles
Wyllys, G. H., 20th Middlesex R.V.

YARROW, A., 21st Middlesex R.V.
Yeatman, C., 1st Middlesex Ryl. Engrs.
York, E. L., 21st Middlesex R.V., d.[2]
York, T., 4th V.B. Essex Regiment
Young, A., 22nd Middlesex R.V.
Young, A., 1st V.B. Essex Rgt., Sergt.
Young, E. A., 2nd V.B. Essex Rgt., d.[3]
Young, G. R., 13th Middlesex R.V.
Young, H., 16th Middx. R.V., L.-Corp.
Young, J., 16th Middlesex R.V.

---

[1] *St. John's, Westminster.* [2] *Congregational Church, Highbury.* [3] *Great Clacton, Essex.*
[a] *West India Regiment.*

APPENDIX I

C.I.V. DRAFT—OFFICERS AND MEN

d. after the name of any man indicates that he died; to all such names is appended a note stating the place where a Memorial has been erected.

BYRNE, Captain S. C., 21st Middlesex R.V.C., with temporary rank of Captain in the Army, 11th July 1900.
CARR, Captain R., 13th Middlesex R.V.C., with temporary rank of Lieutenant in the Army, 11th July 1900.
SELFE, Captain A. A. C., 2nd V.B. Middlesex, with temporary rank of Lieutenant in the Army, 11th July 1900.

ALLEN, H. J., 12th Middx. R.V., Sergt.
Andrews, O. F., 13th Middlesex R.V.
Askew, S. J., 3rd Middlesex V.A.
Auger, F. W., 2nd V.B. Middlesex

BARNARD, W. R., 21st Midx. R.V.
Bassett, R., H.A.C.
Beart, F. C. W., 1st London R.V.
Berry, G. W., 5th Middlesex R.V.
Bertram, A., 7th Middlesex R.V.
Black, R. J., 13th Middlesex R.V.
Bradshaw, C. H., H.A.C.
Bradshaw, R. W., H.A.C.
Bransgrove, S., 1st London R.V.
Brown, A., 21st Middlesex R.V.
Brown, E. K., H.A.C.
Buckle, G. H., 2nd V.B. Middlesex
Butler, W. E., 2nd Kent V.A.
Butterfield, N. W., 13th Midx. R.V.
Byshe, E. H., 1st London R.V.

CANTWELL, G., 21st Middlesex R.V.
Carr, C. A., 13th Middlesex R.V.
Carr, E. N., H.A.C.
Carty, G. H., 1st C.B. King's R.R.
Chambers, E. H., 7th Middlesex R.V.
Chichester, L., 14th Middlesex R.V.
Chillingworth, G., H.A.C., Bombr.
Collins, A., 13th Middlesex R.V.
Collins, B. R., 14th Middlesex R.V.
Colvile, A. G., H.A.C.

Conolly, L. M. U., 1st London R.V.
Cooper, A. M., 2nd Middlesex V.A.
Cooper, H. L., 2nd V.B. Middlesex
Copping, S. O., 4th V. B. East Surrey
Cowan, H. C., 3rd Middlesex V.A.
Cranmer, R., 20th Middlesex R.V.
Crowson, P. W., 1st Tower Hamlets R.V.
Cruse, A. S., 3rd Middlesex V.A.

DANIELL, R. W., 1st Tower Hamlets R.V.
Davis, L. F., 1st Middlesex R.V.
Dawborn, A. W., 4th Middlesex R.V., Sergt., *d.*[1]
Dawes, R. A., 12th Middlesex R.V.
Deane, T. F., 21st Middlesex R.V.
Dorrington, H., 1st Tower Hamlets R.V.
Douet, H. E., 1st London R.V.
Douglas, E. J., 3rd Middlesex V.A.

EDWARDS, J. C., 1st London R.V.
Esterby, G. J., 21st Middlesex R.V.
Eustace, F., 1st London R.V.

FINDEN, G. E., 21st Middlesex R.V.
Flamank, C. J., 13th Middlesex R.V.
Foord, F., 2nd V.B. Middlesex
Forbes, N. D., H.A.C.
Fowler, F., H.A.C.
Franzmann, L., 12th Middlesex R.V.
Fry, W. S., 1st London R.V.

[1] *St. Michael's, Paddington.*

APPENDIX 251

GERAHTY, J. E., 12th Midx. R.V.
Gibson, E. G., 21st Middlesex R.V.
Gillespie, W. R. B., 3rd Lond. R.V., Sgt.
Gisby, D., 2nd V.B. Middlesex
Glenny, J. V., 7th Middlesex R.V.
Glibbery, W. H., 1st Tower Hamlets R.V.
Godwin, R., 21st Middlesex R.V.
Gordon, S. C., 1st London R.V., Sergt.
Griggs, H. A., 21st Middlesex R.V.

HAMMERTON, C. W., 13th Mx. R.V.
Hammerton, H. E., 13th Midx. R.V.
Hammerton, S. C., 13th Midx. R.V.
Hamp, Jun., T. J., H.A.C.
Hampton, G. C., 1st London R.V.
Hart, T. E., 1st London R.V.
Harris, W. H., 21st Middlesex R.V.
Heaford, A. E., 1st Tower Hamlets R.V.
Hickman, F. D., 26th Midx. R.V.
Holmes, W. J., H.A.C.
Houghton, J. G., H.A.C.
Hunt, H. H., 13th Middlesex R.V.
Hurden, A., 13th Middlesex R.V.

JARED, W., 1st Middlesex R.E. Vols.
Jecks, E., 13th Middlesex R.V.
Johnson, G. F. G., 7th Midx. R.V.
Jolliffe, B. J., 12th Middlesex R.V.
Jones, H. E., 1st Tow. Hamlets R.V.
Jones, S. C., H.A.C.
Jordan, F. L., 1st T. Hamlets R.V.
Josephs, P. R. E., 1st London R.V.

LADENBURG, A. L., H.A.C.
Layton, E., 7th Middlesex R.V.
Lewis, B. R., 13th Middlesex R.V.
Lintott, A. J. C., 1st London R.V.
Luckett, T. McA., 5th Midx. R.V.

McDONELL, F. H., 1st C.B. King's R.R.
McKechnie, E. A., H.A.C.
Melsom, F. A., 3rd Middlesex V.A.
Messer, C. W., 20th Middlesex R.V.
Methven, J. McL., 7th Middx. R.V.
Miller, E. J., 12th Middlesex R.V.
Morcom, A. B., H.A.C.
Murcott, C. W., 13th Middlesex R.V.

NEWNHAM, A. G., 7th Middlesex R.V.
Noakes, C. E., 13th Middlesex R.V.

OPPENHEIM, J., H.A.C.

PAINE, C. H., H.A.C.
Palmer, F., 2nd V.B. Middlesex
Pateman, A. A., 1st T. Hamlets R.V.
Pattrick, J. W., 1st V.B. Essex Regt.

RAMSEY, H. V., H.A.C.
Ranwell, W. G., 21st Middlesex R.V.
Rawlings, F. C., 2nd V.B. Midx., d.[1]
Rayfield, E., 21st Middlesex R.V.
Reid, A. V., 26th Middlesex R.V.
Richardson, A. F., 1st Tower Hamlets R.V.
Robinson, R. W., 7th Middlesex R.V.
Rogers, A. H., 20th Middlesex R.V.
Rolfe, A. E., 3rd Middlesex V.A.
Rolls, E. F., 12th Middlesex R.V.
Runford, A. R., 13th Middlesex R.V.
Rumsey, G. H., 13th Middlesex R.V.
Rusby, L. H., H.A.C.
Russell, E., 7th Middlesex R.V.

SAUNDERS, J., 2nd V.B. Middlesex
Short, R. T., 5th Middlesex R.V.
Smith, H. W., 21st Middlesex R.V.
Smith, J. H., 13th Middlesex R.V.
Sparks, R. J., 12th Middlesex R.V.
Stacey, T. E., 5th Middlesex R.V.
Strike, A. V., 1st Tower Hamlets R.V.
Sweetingham, T., 1st Tower Hamlets R.V.

TANNER, G. D., 1st Middlesex R.V.
Tibbles, J., 1st Middlesex R.V.
Titley, P., 1st London R.V.
Trapp, H. G., H.A.C.
Treasure, A., 21st Middlesex R.V.
Tremearne, R. H., H.A.C.

VELLENOWETH, A., 1st London R.V.

WALLACE, A., 21st Middlesex R.V.
Watters, R. B., 4th Middlesex R.V.
Webster, M. P., H.A.C.
Welsby, F. H., 13th Middx. R.V., d.[2]
Wildman, J. T., 21st Middx. R.V., Sgt.
Wilkinson, J. C., 2nd V.B. Middlesex
Williams, B., H.A.C.
Williams, J. W., 21st Middlesex R.V.
Wisdom, H. T., 2nd V.B. Middlesex
Wolfe, W. J., 21st Middlesex R.V.
Woodward, S. A., 13th Middx. R.V.
Woolner, R. A., H.A.C.
Wootton, H. E., 5th Middlesex R.V.

---

[1] *Not settled.* [2] *Westminster Abbey.*

APPENDIX K[1]

CITY OF LONDON IMPERIAL VOLUNTEERS

The number of officers and men who served in South Africa is as follows :—

Officers.	Other Ranks.	Total.
64	1675	1739

Of whom—

	Officers.	Other Ranks.	Total.
Killed and died	1	60	61
Wounded	1	60	61
Invalided	5	150	155
Sick in South Africa	—	48	48
Government employ, discharged, &c., in South Africa	2	119	121
Resigned	1	—	1
Given commission	6	25	31
On board *Aurania*	48	1275	1323
On leave to England	2	—	2
	65[2]	1677[3]	1742

[1] This return was made on the 29th October 1900.
[2] One officer is shown in two columns, viz., "Given commission" and "On board."
[3] Two men appear in "Given commission" and "On board."
Wounded not included in the addition.

www.ingramcontent.com/pod-product-compliance
Lightning Source LLC
Chambersburg PA
CBHW031135160426
43193CB00008B/142